SALISBURY

The History of an English Cathedral City

SALISBURY

The History of an English Cathedral City

DAVID BURNETT

Compton Press

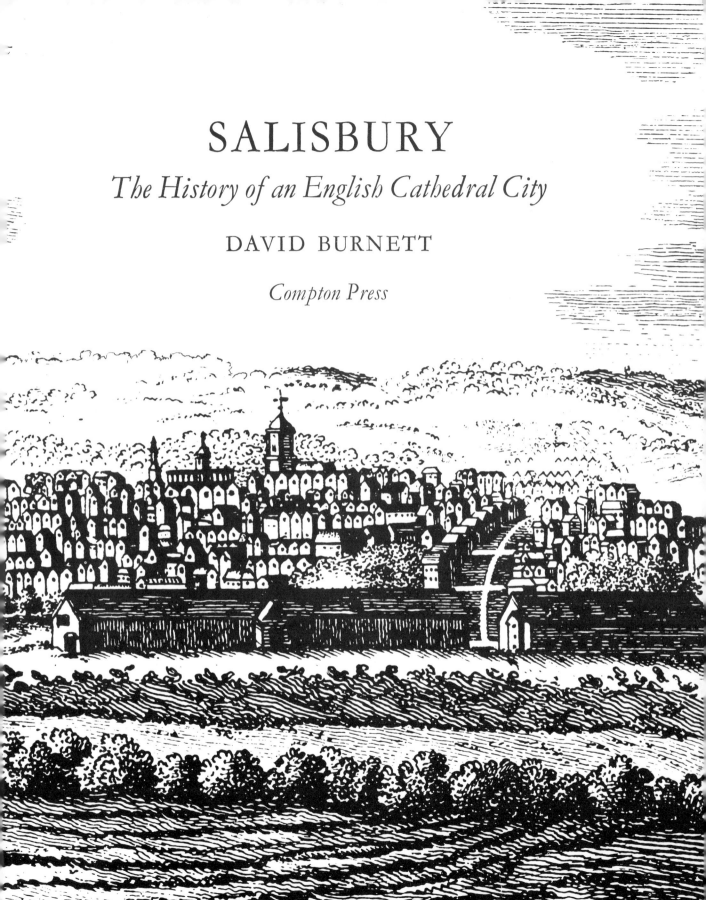

Acknowledgements

I am grateful to the following for allowing me to make use of the illustrations in this book: Wiltshire Library & Museum Service, Salisbury Divisional Library, pages 2, 13 (Aerofilms Ltd), 24, 25, 25, 26, 27, 28, 29, 32, 41, 45, 52, 54, 63, 64, 65, 68, 74, 75, 76, 79; Salisbury & South Wiltshire Museum, 8, 11, 14, 34, 36, 39, 46, 47, 69, 69, 73, 80, 86; The Chief Executive, Salisbury District Council, 82, 85; The Wiltshire Archaeological Society, 30, 30, 31, 33, 35, 40, 56, 58, 61, 63, 64, 67, 68, 69, 70, 70, 72, 72, 73, 74, 83, 84, 89; Antony Miles Ltd, 16, 19, 21, 21, 22; The David J. N. Pennels Collection, 88, 88. (David Burnett, 18, 23, 23, 24, 47, 55, 62, 66, 73.) I am also grateful to the following for allowing me to quote copyright passages: Messrs. Faber & Faber Ltd (William Golding's *The Spire*); Penguin Books Ltd (J. H. Plumb's *England in the Eighteenth Century*).

c. 1940?

© David Burnett
First published by The Compton Press Ltd.
The Old Brewery, Tisbury, Wilts

Set in Linotype Granjon
and printed by Optima Print & Packaging Ltd.

Designed by Humphrey Stone
at The Compton Press Ltd.

ISBN 0 900193 54 9

Contents

Preface

When it was first suggested that I write a history of Old Sarum and Salisbury I had only a vague idea as to where research might lead me, and none as to how enjoyable the journey would become. At the time I was uneasy. I feared that the city's history might prove uninteresting, that the placid respectability of its present might characterize its past. I was mistaken, but for beliefs such as these – which are commonplace – the twentieth century is partly to blame. For paradoxically, although we live in an age of change the contemporary history of the English cathedral city has little to commend it to those who hope for more than a record of municipal improvement in their reading of local history. We have grown so used to worrying about traffic congestion, the need for preservation of listed buildings, the siting of new housing developments, that we all too easily assume that such matters have always dominated urban life. In some ways they have, but the debate over the siting of a new car park is a far cry from the medieval ordinance requesting the population of Salisbury to prevent their pigs and poultry from scavenging through the refuse in the city street channels. The same is true of the cathedral. Who, on entering it today, would believe that the clergy once flighted their hawks at the pigeons roosting in the nave.

Salisbury's history must be amongst the most absorbing and remarkable of any English city. Always invigorating and surprising, often thought-provoking, it reveals much about the character and preoccupations of the nameless priests, merchants and craftsmen who once lived and worked within its ramparts. The strain of eccentricity that runs through so much of its past has, alas, been dissipated, but without it the city could never have assumed its present importance as a centre of worship and trade. The sense of discovery which stayed with me when writing this book is a tribute to the richness and diversity of the city's history, and if I have done less than justice to those who shaped it I can only hope that I have left some signposts along the way.

This book is not intended as an academic guide to Salisbury and its architecture. That path has been well-trodden and in a sense I am reaping the harvest of all those who have already written on some aspect of Salisbury or its history. In a text of this length it seemed unnecessary to include footnotes, but their absence does not detract from my debt to all those whose work I consulted when writing and thinking about Salisbury. All the main sources are listed in the brief bibliography on page 92 .

I am deeply grateful to Edward Boyle and the staff of Salisbury Reference

Library for their kindness; without this assistance, the difficulties inherent in any research would have been far greater. I am also indebted to Miss P. A. Rundle, Keeper of the Muniments, Salisbury District Council; David Pennels; Antony Miles; Peter Saunders and Tiffany Hunt of the Salisbury and South Wiltshire Museum; and Richard Sandell and David Mansfield of the Wiltshire Archaelogical Society for allowing me to make use of illustrations in their possession.

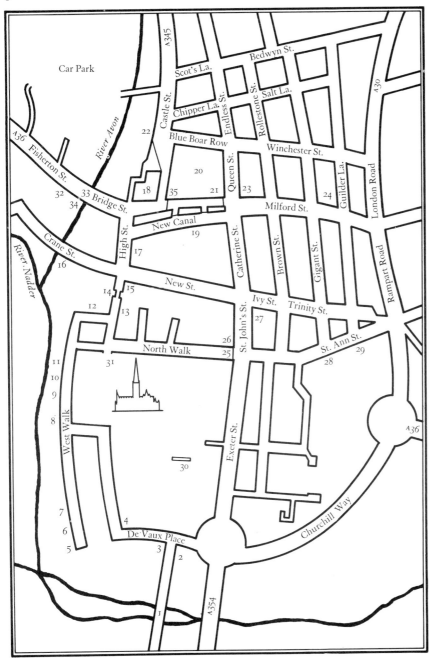

1 Ayleswade Bridge and St. John's Chapel
2 St. Nicholas's Hospital
3 College of St. Nicholas de Vaux
4 Harnham Gate
5 South Canonry
6 Leadenhall
7 Walton Canonry
8 King's House
9 North Canonry
10 Arundells
11 Wardrobe
12 Mompesson House
13 College of Matrons
14 High Street Gate
15 Mitre House
16 Church House
17 Old George Inn
18 St. Thomas's Church
19 John Hall's house
20 Market Place
21 Guildhall
22 Central Library
23 John a'Porte's house
24 Tailors' Hall
25 St. Ann's Gate
26 Malmesbury House
27 White Hart
28 Museum
29 Joiners' Hall
30 Bishop's Palace
31 Town Mills
32 Infirmary
33 Fisherton Bridge
34 Site of Gaol
35 Poultry Cross

ONE

Old Sarum

... to it and in it; and find it so prodigious so as to fright me to be in it all alone at that time of night, it being dark. I understand since it to be that that is called Old Sarum.

SAMUEL PEPYS 1668

Towards the end of the 1890s a party of tourists alighted at Salisbury's Fisherton Street station from the London train, hired a hansom cab and ordered the driver to take them on a tour of the city. He took them first not to the Close, cathedral or Market Place, but to the new gasworks which had recently been built in a northern suburb. Their fate was not typical, but it does hint at one of the underlying themes in Salisbury's history: the urban pride of its citizens. During the nineteenth century the flow of visitors to Salisbury had gradually increased. Some came to admire the cathedral, others on business, whilst Mr. Pecksniff's architectural students in *Martin Chuzzlewit* spent the five years that followed their arrival 'making elevations of Salisbury Cathedral from every possible point of sight'. Dickens could have chosen no apter image, for by the middle of the century the cathedral was amongst the most celebrated in England, a visible summary of the national achievement. Yet those who then lived in its shadow seem to have regarded it with as much indifference as they did pride. Indeed, after an irreverent Victorian city draper had been ordered not to climb the spire, he went ahead and did so, afterwards rejecting an admiring tourist's offer of £2 for his trousers on the grounds that it was an insult to the cathedral; a contradiction so subtle that no magistrate dared fine him for fear of being mobbed!

These brief nineteenth century *vignettes* of Salisbury life are indicative of the attitudes that have shaped its history. For although its physical and architectural attractions are obvious, the achievements of those who founded, built and lived in the city are too easily ignored. Bishops, merchants, drunkards, whores; the full range of man's virtues and vices, Salisbury's story contains them all. It could never have developed into the prosperous and self-contained English cathedral city that it is today without the vision and independence of its citizens. The foundation of the city was a unique experiment in medieval town planning and the construction of the cathedral a triumph of local craftsmanship and Christian faith. But without the perseverance of the bishops who have held the see, the ambition of its mayors and merchants, and the talent of the apprentices and tradesmen who once crowded its streets,

Old Sarum, a detail from the painting by John Constable.

9

Salisbury could never have acquired its present character. 800 years ago the city did not exist. The open ditches that gave Salisbury an undeserved reputation for being an English Venice had neither been dug, nor filled in. Dickens had not created the ubiquitous Pecksniff. The cathedral spire had not been built and the gasworks would have bewildered the Fisherton miller who then occupied one of the only buildings on the site of the modern city.

Salisbury's history begins on a windswept and desolate hill known as Old Sarum, two miles to the north of the existing city. Today the hill is uninhabited, but prior to the thirteenth century, it was a thriving town with a cathedral and castle and a history that predated Roman Britain. Old Sarum was probably first settled three centuries before the birth of Christ by the Iron Age tribesmen who roamed the chalk downlands of southern Wiltshire. Circular earthworks were dug and the site became a hill-fort with commanding views over the ancient tracks that crossed the Avon, Nadder and Wylye rivers. The sparse vegetation of the neighbouring downs provided pasture for sheep, the earthworks offered safety against attack, and its position on the well-watered southern rim of Salisbury Plain contrasted favourably with the bleak wilderness to the north and the dense woodland which then cloaked much of the surrounding countryside.

Old Sarum's settlement took place towards the end of the early history of Wessex. The area had long been attractive to primitive man. Stonehenge is eight miles to the north, Avebury thirty, and the burial mounds, barrows, sacred circles and standing stones left behind by earlier settlers span 2,500 years of prehistory. Old Sarum's accessibility attracted traders from other settlements in Wessex. Traders from Glastonbury lake-village left behind a bronze belt-link, excavated from a refuse pit on the site. Pottery, brooches and coins belonging to the Belgic tribes who invaded southern England in the first century B.C. have also been found.

The defensive and strategic position of Old Sarum contributed to its development. It had access to water and potential farmland, and the combination of a landscape characterized by rolling downland and fertile river valleys made it a natural stronghold. To the west the ground slopes gently down to the River Avon, but to the east and north it falls sharply to the Plain, making defence much easier. The proximity of the Avon was vital to Old Sarum. For within view of the hill-fort the Avon's flow is augmented by the Nadder, Wylye, Bourne and Ebble rivers, and it then flows south to join the sea in Christchurch harbour. The existence of these rivers, one of them navigable, with their fords and crossing places, added to Old Sarum's importance as a trading centre and fortified camp.

After the Roman invasion Old Sarum became a military town called Sorviodonum. Any baths, barracks, villas or temples built by the Romans were probably situated to the west of the central ramparts, and the later Saxon village of Stratford-sub-Castle indicates where the Roman 'street' forded the river. Sorviodonum's position made it an obvious junction for the system of roads by which the Romans kept a conquered country under control. To the west ran the main highways to Dorchester, the Bristol Channel and the Mendip lead mines. Others went east to Winchester and north-east to the now deserted city of Silchester. Many of these roads have survived and sections are still in use.

After the final collapse of Roman Britain Old Sarum's development was temporarily halted and both the hill-fort and town may have been abandoned. The area was re-occupied by the native Britons and it was they who attempted to halt the invasion of Wessex by the Anglo-Saxons in the sixth century. Their efforts met with little success and the capture of Old Sarum by the West Saxons in 552 marks the beginning of Anglo-Saxon settlement in southern Wiltshire. Although the Saxons re-named the hill Searoburh or the 'place of battle' they never regarded it as suitable for settlement. Instead they established their farms and homesteads in the surrounding river valleys, and many of the small villages that line the Nadder, Wylye and Avon are Saxon in origin. The water meadows offered grazing for cattle, the valley slopes were easily cultivated, and the higher downland provided pasture for sheep. The way of life enjoyed by the new colonists was essentially pastoral, and, although the local town of Wilton became a provincial capital for the Saxon kings of Wessex, the re-occupation of Old Sarum was delayed until the beginning of the Danish invasions in the ninth century. During a brief truce between Alfred and the Danes its outer ditch was re-dug and the earthworks lined with palisades. A century later it was the scene of a council meeting called by Edgar to discuss how best to defend Wessex against Viking attack. But nothing could be done to halt the Danish advance and in 1003 Wilton was sacked, its mint destroyed and three of its four moneyers were forced to take refuge in Old Sarum.

Roman pottery excavated from Old Sarum.

By the date of the Norman Conquest in 1066 Old Sarum, or Sarisberie as it was called in the Anglo-Saxon Chronicle, had grown into a small but flourishing town. It was still a defensive outpost to Wilton, but its earthworks were intact and it boasted its own mint. The Domesday Book records the existence of four mills along the Avon and a small township had sprung up on the sloping ground to the south and west of the main ramparts.

Shortly after the Norman invasion the town was re-named Salisberie. William I ordered a wooden castle to be built on a man-made mound in the centre of the earthworks, the moat was deepened and the outer defences strengthened. Old Sarum's position and the closeness of the royal hunting palace at Clarendon added to its prestige and the new castle was granted to the Sheriffs of Wiltshire. In 1075 Bishop Herman of Sherborne transferred his see (which then covered much of Wiltshire, Dorset, Berkshire and Hampshire) to the hill-top and began the construction of a cathedral to the north of the castle. This decision, which forced the clergy and military garrison to share the limited acreage of the original fort, was to result in Old Sarum's ruin and the foundation of modern Salisbury. The new cathedral was built in an obscure architectural style. Shaped like a small basilica, with as eastern apse and two transeptal towers, it owed less to Saxon or Norman design than Herman's Rhineland origins. Shortly after its consecration by his successor, Bishop Osmund, in 1092, it was struck by lightning and the eastern end was severely damaged.

The appointment of Osmund to Salisbury led to a major change in the city's fortunes. Born illegitimate, once William's chancellor, a crown servant whose greatest pleasure lay in binding and illuminating medieval manuscripts, Osmund's episcopacy marks the start of Salisbury's rise. William II granted him a local manor of some 5,000 acres and its income was used to consolidate the position of the church. He established a cathedral chapter with a dean and secular canons, an innovation which later became common throughout England. The foundation of the chapter attracted additional clergy to the city, and houses were built for them between the castle and outer defences. Osmund also formed the nucleus of the cathedral library and evolved the order for the performance of services which eventually developed into the famous Sarum Rite. The Sarum Rite was later to be widely imitated throughout Europe and it added to the cathedral's reputation as a centre of worship and religious study. Osmund remains a saintly but half-legendary figure. He was described by a contemporary as free of ambition and renowned for his charity. He died in 1099 and a stone bearing that date, which is thought to have been placed over his grave, is now in Salisbury Cathedral. He was accredited with several miracles, legends collected round his memory, and, in 1457, after prolonged and costly negotiations with the Vatican – 'for when the sound of money ceases the dispatch of business ceases also' – he was canonized and named patron saint of Salisbury.

Osmund's successor was cast in a different mould. Roger of Caen was unscrupulous, ambitious, self-made and the first of many medieval officials who managed to combine spiritual office with secular power. Several of his biographers insist that he owed his rise to the speed with which he read mass before a royal hunting expedition. His indifference to liturgical niceties was later rewarded and when Henry I became king in 1100 he was appointed Chancellor of England; two years later he was created Bishop of Salisbury.

Central to Roger's character was a passion for architecture and he at once set to work re-designing the damaged cathedral. The transeptal towers were demolished and replaced by a central tower, the choir was lengthened, and aisled transepts and two western towers added. Today, only the bare outline of the foundations remain, but the original building, standing solitary and magnificent on the heights of Old Sarum, must have been an impressive symbol of the power of the Norman church. Roger's obsession with buildings was not easily satisfied and, after first obtaining the governorship of the castle, he rebuilt it. Once again only the foundations and a few fragments of the inner masonry remain, but it seems certain that the second castle consisted of a central courtyard surrounded by a rectangular keep. As Roger was both castellan of the castle and Bishop of Sarum he transformed it

Old Sarum from the air. The ramparts mark the extent of the old city; the central mound contains the remains of the Norman castle; the cathedral foundations are on the right.

Fragments of carved masonry found on the site of Old Sarum Cathedral. The cathedral was designed by Bishop Herman (1075–1078), completed by his successor Bishop Osmund (1078–1099), and rebuilt by Bishop Roger (1102–1139).

into a fortified palace. The construction of a bishop's palace became unnecessary and he turned his attentions to the building of three further castles, at Devizes, Sherborne and Malmesbury; none of which survive in their original form.

Roger's political ambitions never dimmed, and after Henry I's death he betrayed the king's daughter and sided with Stephen in the struggle for the crown. The bishop's change of loyalty was too sudden and too unlikely to satisfy Stephen and he was imprisoned in Devizes Castle. Deprived of his property, disgraced and broken, he was eventually permitted to return to Old Sarum. His treatment (an account of his career mentions three days' starvation and imprisonment in a cowshed hay-rack) and the inconsistency of royal favours seem to have unnerved him. One medieval chronicler relates that prior to his death he began 'raving and taking on like a man distrait of his wits.'

The misfortunes of its bishop failed to hinder Old Sarum's growth. The establishment of the cathedral and castle had added to its population and prosperity. Roger granted it an annual fair and excused its citizens from paying tolls, both of which increased its commercial importance. Old Sarum was one of the few medieval hill towns in southern England (Shaftesbury, 20 miles to the west, is another) and the lack of space meant that most of the townspeople lived in suburbs outside the eastern and western gates. The eastern settlement supported its own parish church and the houses to the west stretched down towards the Avon and the village of Stratford-sub-Castle. Here the villagers' open-field plots intermingled with the allotments leased by the townspeople from the bishop. The city's commercial heart was contained within the Iron Age ramparts, where the garrison and cathedral servants were also housed. The existence of a cathedral within a fortress led to frequent clashes between the military and the clergy. Brawls and bloodshed were common and on one occasion the entire cathedral chapter was locked out of the city at night after returning from a nearby church.

In the early thirteenth century the episcopate was held by two brothers, Herbert and Richard Poore. It was probably Herbert who first considered moving the cathedral and in 1217 his brother Richard obtained permission to abandon Old Sarum and build a new cathedral on 'spacious fields of pleasantness' alongside the Avon to the south of the city. Two years later the ground was consecrated and a wooden chapel built on the site. Bishop Poore's reasons for wishing to evacuate Old Sarum were listed in a papal enquiry. The attitude of the garrison towards the clergy was so hostile that those hoping to visit the cathedral were often prevented from entering the city. The cathedral was in danger of collapsing and the congregation was so small that there were barely enough funds for the maintenance of the roof. There were insufficient houses for the clergy and no room for new ones. Water was constantly in short supply; it had to be carted in, at a price, and the carters had to obtain their licences from the castle governor. Some of the additional complaints lodged by the cathedral chapter are imaginative but unconvincing. The glare from the chalk caused blindness, the exposed position of the cathedral encouraged rheumatism and high winds drowned the choristers' voices and made prayer pointless. The improbability of some of these latter grievances obscure Old Sarum's very real disadvantages. The relationship between the governor and bishop was too uncertain to attract trade. Economic growth depends on stability and room for expansion, and Old Sarum lacked both. The Poore brothers had realized that although the cathedral owned much of the land surrounding the city, it did not own the city itself, and without adding to its rents and increasing its income its position would remain precarious. A combination of common sense and financial necessity made a move inevitable and, in 1220, when a barefooted Bishop Poore laid the foundation stone of the new cathedral on its existing site, the history of modern Salisbury had begun.

After its evacuation by the clergy Old Sarum was gradually abandoned. The Sheriffs of Wiltshire continued to occupy and maintain the castle, but by the mid-thirteenth century it had been turned into a prison. In 1300 the prisoners were being kept in a room whose ceiling was so rotten that its collapse was expected daily. Five years later twenty of them broke out, killed a sheriff's clerk and removed some of the royal treasure stored in the castle before making their escape. The cathedral was demolished in the fourteenth century and its stone incorporated into the Close wall. When Leland visited the hill in 1535 he found the city uninhabited, no evidence of the cathedral, and 'much notable ruinous building' of the castle.

Even as a dead city Old Sarum's name lingered on. As the rottenest of Rotten Boroughs it continued to elect two Members of Parliament until the Reform Act of 1832. At the 1816 election the electorate consisted of seven voters and, although William Pitt the elder had first sat as Member for Old Sarum, the citizens of Salisbury celebrated the Reform Act of 1832 with bonfires and a public dinner. William Cobbett, the Radical M.P., turned his head when passing the 'Accursed Hill' on his rural ride down the Avon valley. Ironically, shortly after 1832, part of the huge elm under which the elections had taken place, blew down. With that Old Sarum became the deserted and windswept hill that survives today.

TWO

Beginning Again, the Cathedral and Close

I have been credibly informed that some foreign artists beholding this building break forth into tears ... grieving that they
had not the like in their own land.

THOMAS FULLER *The Worthies of England*

The medieval church acted as the link between man's life on earth and his
conviction that death was followed by eternal life. The concept of a planet
revolving in space was unthinkable, the oceans were uncharted, the earth's
geography was a mystery, and most men and women lived and died in the
village of their birth. In an uncertain world where God could summon up
apparitions, visions, plagues, storms, and miracles to bear witness to His
existence, the church represented order and security. Thirteenth century man
believed that the universe was governed by a divine law which the church
interpreted on his behalf, helped him to obey, and obtained forgiveness for
him when he broke it. He was baptized, married and buried by God's representatives on earth. He turned to them to plead a cure for his ills, to offer
penance and to pray for forgiveness and comfort. The construction of Salisbury Cathedral was made possible by the extraordinary power that the
church had over men's souls. There was no doubting the articles of Chris-
tion faith. Life was short, filled with hardship, poverty and sickness, and all
men accepted without question a religion that embraced their anxieties and
fears, made room for success and failure, and offered the possibility of eternal
salvation.

This straightforward acceptance of life after death is at the heart of the
medieval attitude to religion. Endowments by the wealthy, the alms given by
the poor, were all intended to obtain absolution from sin and prevent death
being followed by damnation. The money and land given to the church
added to its power and turned it into a visible symbol of God's authority on
earth. The great medieval Gothic cathedrals of England were amongst the
sole centres of learning, they attracted pilgrims and trade, their architecture
depicted a simple morality in glass, timber and stone, and their clergy, from
bishop down to parish priest, held the keys to Heaven and Hell.

By the date of Bishop Poore's decision to abandon Old Sarum the church
had outgrown its missionary origins. Its cathedrals were situated in the

Salisbury Cathedral floodlit at
night.

17

Salisbury Cathedral, the west front. Richard Poore, Bishop of Salisbury (1217–1229), holding a model of the cathedral.

centres of population and its wealth was immense. Its bishops were feudal magnates who were answerable only to the king, their archbishop, the pope and God. They headed a complex hierarchy of cathedral dignitaries of whom the most important, the dean, was responsible for its maintenance and administration. The other leading officials were the treasurer, chancellor – responsible for the library and education of the clergy, and the precentor, who supervised the singing and conduct of services. The establishment of the chapter had led to the appointment of canons, each of whom was assigned a portion of its revenue as a stipend. Osmund had intended that the principal dignitaries should always be in residence, 'putting away all thoughts of absence,' but many of them were irregular participants in an exacting routine of worship which began with matins at five o'clock, continued almost without pause until noon, and ended with vespers and compline in the evening. Many canons were rich laymen and their appointment was a reward for service to the crown. When absent their duties were performed by singing vicars, the vicars choral. Around the cathedral orbited an entire army of lesser officials. The bishop was assisted in his diocesan work by archdeacons and rural deans. Choristers, servers, sextons, clerks, monks, librarians, the ecclesiastical lawyers who administered its courts, all played their part in the observance of an elaborate and ritualistic way of life. At the heyday of the medieval church one in thirty of the adult males in Western Europe was a cleric of some kind. Each of these officials needed lodgings, and the building in which they worshipped had to offer proof of their authority and the all-embracing influence of the Christian faith. It was with these considerations in mind that Bishop Poore began planning the design of the cathedral and the layout of the Close.

The ground chosen for the site of the new cathedral was well-watered and flat and there was ample space for both a cathedral Close and the foundation of a new city. Poore was a realist, he understood that the cathedral's independence depended on its ability to attract trade and raise money from a market and urban rents. The city was conceived with two distinct quarters: the ecclesiastical, centred round the cathedral and contained by the Close ditches, and a commercial quarter based on the Market Place. It was an ambitious scheme, but it is the relationship between the two areas of the city that gives Salisbury its character and makes it so remarkable an example of medieval town planning.

The task of translating Poore's vision into a reality was undertaken by one of the canons, Elias of Dereham, an honest and distinguished administrator who had worked with three Archbishops of Canterbury, the Bishops of Wells, Lincoln and Winchester and who had helped design Becket's shrine at Canterbury. It was he who drew the initial plans of the cathedral, as a cross with two pairs of arms as transepts, and who built Leadenhall, in the West Walk of the Close, as a model for the other canons' houses. The first five stones were laid in 1220, three by Bishop Poore, the fourth by Wil-

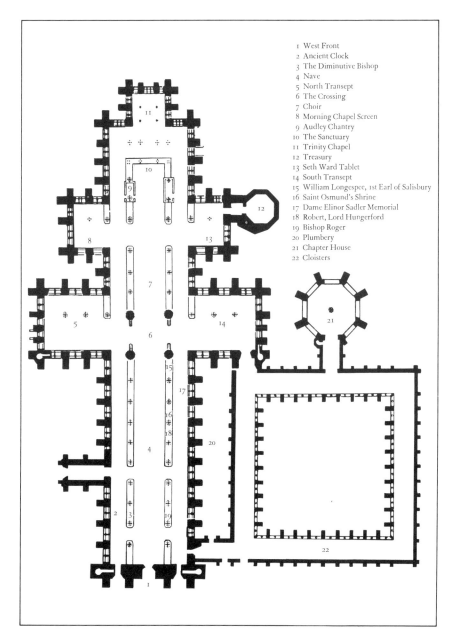

1 West Front
2 Ancient Clock
3 The Diminutive Bishop
4 Nave
5 North Transept
6 The Crossing
7 Choir
8 Morning Chapel Screen
9 Audley Chantry
10 The Sanctuary
11 Trinity Chapel
12 Treasury
13 Seth Ward Tablet
14 South Transept
15 William Longespee, 1st Earl of Salisbury
16 Saint Osmund's Shrine
17 Dame Elinor Sadler Memorial
18 Robert, Lord Hungerford
19 Bishop Roger
20 Plumbery
21 Chapter House
22 Cloisters

The stone figure of Elias of Dereham. The figure, which stands at the foot of the main pillar in the south aisle, was given to the cathedral by the Free-masons of Salisbury in 1946.

liam Longspee, Earl of Salisbury, one of the signatories of Magna Carta and whose copy, one of only four in existence, is still preserved in the cathedral library, and the fifth by his wife. Five years later the earl returned to England from France to die and was buried in a tomb designed by Elias of Dereham in the cathedral he had helped found. That autumn the first completed part of the new building, the Trinity Chapel, was dedicated by Cardinal Langton, and in the following year the bodies of three of the bishops of Old Sarum, Osmund amongst them, were brought down and re-interred in the new cathedral.

Salisbury Cathedral owes its construction to English muscle. The building team was headed by Nicholas of Ely, the master mason, and it was he who supervised the hundreds of labourers employed on the site. The leading craftsmen were the freemasons, who travelled in small bands in search of work and whose lean-to 'lodges', erected as temporary shelter, still survive in the language of freemasonry. It was they who trimmed and dressed the great blocks of limestone, hauled by oxen from quarries at Chilmark, ten miles west of Salisbury, with which the cathedral is built. They were assisted in their work by gangs of lime-burners, carters, joiners, wrights, slaters, sculptors, glaziers, plumbers and turners – the last of whom used primitive stone lathes to shape the forest of delicate columns and pillars that fill the interior.

For the twenty years that followed the dedication of the Trinity Chapel the new building rose slowly within its web of wooden scaffolding. Squares and plumb-lines ensured its accuracy and proportion. The oak timbers that knitted the fabric together were hauled into place with block and tackle. Wicker baskets lifted the slates, lead and mortar high into the soaring skeleton of the uncompleted building. The workmen's wages were low, conditions hard, and even though the masons were granted indulgences, or remission of penance for sins, which the church conferred on the rich and powerful, nothing prevented disputes. On one occasion the masons went on strike to have their daily wages raised to $1\frac{1}{4}$d.; the meadows where they camped are now part of Pennyfarthing Street.

The task of raising the money to pay for the work was entrusted to the treasurer, the saintly Edmund Rich, later Archbishop of Canterbury. The canons were forced to pay part of their stipend into the building fund and those that refused had their corn seized. Members of the chapter travelled as far afield as Ireland to preach and gather alms. Local landowners and merchants made endowments, a twelve year supply of Purbeck marble was given and chantries were established – in which, in return for payment, chaplains prayed for the founder's soul. Salisbury Cathedral is dedicated to Our Lady, the Blessed Virgin Mary, and the womanly virtues of charity, pity and compassion expressed in that dedication do much to explain the enormous gifts that allowed its construction. Henry III, the greatest patron of ecclesiastical architecture England has ever known, was a regular visitor to the site, riding over from his hunting palace at Clarendon, only 2 miles to the east of the city. It was he who gave the massive timbers used in the tower and roof and by 1258, when the cathedral was consecrated in his presence, the transepts, nave and choir had all been completed. Within ten years the west front had been added and by the end of the century the cloisters and chapter house had been built in the shelter of the south wall.

Salisbury Cathedral, apart from the upper tower and spire which were added later, is the essence of Early English Gothic architecture. Vaulting space with stone, a vision of height, light and energy, the unity of its design owes much to the uninterrupted nature of the work. The ordered existence

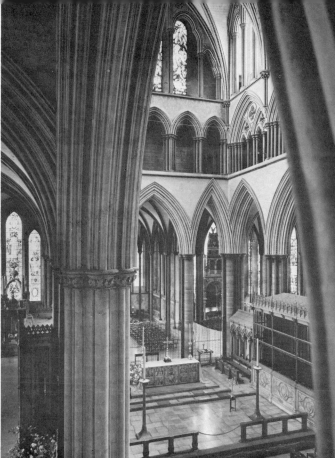

in which its builders believed is fundamental to its character. The pillars rising like trees from flagstone floors, the foliage-carved walls and arches, the light flooding in through tiers of lancet windows, the then gilded capitals on the shafts and mouldings, the choir ceiling depicting the seasonal tasks of rural life – beginning with the labourer warming his hands before the fire and ending with the slaughter of the Christmas pig – the then brightly painted walls decorated with black scroll work; each of these images symbolized the unity between heaven and earth so essential to a people whose world was bounded by sky and rolling downland.

The cathedral's interior has been much 'improved' since the end of the thirteenth century and it is hard to imagine it at the moment of initial completion. But gazing down its 449 foot length one is aware of its slenderness and simplicity. The tombs and effigies gathered in the side aisles, the lines of Chilmark columns rising up to the vaulted ceiling, the Trinity Chapel with its narrow, pointed arches and roof balanced on slender pillars of polished Purbeck marble, emphasize the contrast between colour, light and stone. The aspiring spirit of the Gothic is still tempered by the delicacy of traditional design. Ornament was used only sparingly and the interior's clarity remains its most impressive legacy. The choir was originally divided from the nave by a stone screen, but only a portion of this survives, set into the wall in the Morning Chapel. The tombs, shrines, effigies and chapels now ranged

LEFT Salisbury Cathedral, looking west along the nave.

RIGHT Salisbury Cathedral, the sanctuary. Beyond the alter screen can be seen part of the Lady Chapel, now known as the Trinity Chapel.

along the aisles and transepts were built gradually in memory of Salisbury's bishops and the local nobility. Typical of these is the tomb of Giles de Bridport, bishop when the cathedral was consecrated, whose tomb in the south aisle, once enclosed by a chantry chapel, is covered with a stone canopy carved with scenes from his life.

The chapter house, cloisters and west front were all completed by Nicholas of Ely's successor, Richard the mason. The west front is an eccentric departure from the remainder of the exterior. Compared to the immense ribbed flank of the rest of the cathedral, which extends along the Close lawns and is broken by three tiers of windows, the west front is complex and elaborate. It was built to display the large numbers of sculpted figures that now occupy its niches, the window was only constituted in its present form in 1894, and the small west door seems out of proportion to the towering façade. Richard the mason's best work is to be found in the chapter house and cloisters. The latter have suffered badly from neglect and are at present being restored. But their clustered shafts and arches, their endless mouldings receding in perspec-

Salisbury Cathedral, the west walk of the cloisters. Each of the four cloister walks, the largest in the country, is 181 feet long. They were started in 1263, five years after the consecration of the cathedral.

Salisbury Cathedral, the west front.

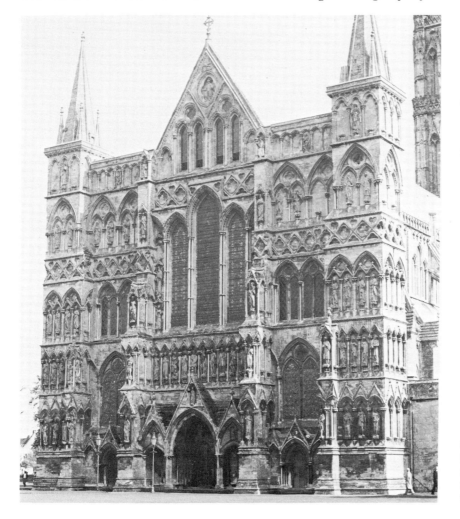

OPPOSITE
Salisbury Cathedral, the late fourteenth century strainer arch at the entrance to the north choir transept.

23

Salisbury Cathedral, the interior of the chapter house looking west into the cloisters. The geometric windows are similar in design to the cloister arcades.

Salisbury Cathedral, the north wall of the Chapter House, Noah in his Vineyard.

tive under the interarchings of the roof and the patterns of sunlight and shadow that fill the alleys make them a superb example of the imagination and technique that is the hallmark of the best medieval craftsmen. The octagonal chapter house, built as a conference chamber for the canons, with its fan vaulted ceiling supported by a single column, extends the cathedral's sense of space. A stone plinth with seats for the canons circles the walls. Below the windows are sculpted faces and a series of bas-reliefs telling Old Testament stories. Over the doorway a further set of fourteen sculptures show the triumph of Virtue over Vice; the images of Sobriety dowsing Drunkenness, of Truth drawing the tongue of Falsehood, must, on occasions, have served as a timely reminder to the dean and chapter to practise as they preached.

In 1334, more than a century after the laying of the foundation stones, work began on Salisbury's most famous landmark – the cathedral spire. What prompted its construction remains unknown, but William Golding's

24

Salisbury Cathedral, a view from the south into the north transept. This eighteenth century engraving shows the two girder-arches built, circa 1460, on either side of the crossing to stabilise the tower piers.

Salisbury Cathedral, an eighteenth century engraving of part of the cathedral, showing the interior of the tower and spire.

novel *The Spire*, published in 1964, provides a vivid portrait of the doubts and conflicts that must have marked its rise. Golding never mentions Salisbury by name, but he was for many years a master at Bishop Wordsworth's school and it seems probable that the spire's construction inspired the novel. 'In this house . . .', says the fictional dean in *The Spire*, 'we have woven a rich fabric of constant praise. Things shall be as they were: only better, richer, the pattern of worship complete at last.' No other motive has as yet been suggested for an achievement that reflects all the folly, grandeur, creativity and vain glory of the age in which it was built.

Salisbury Cathedral had been left with only a squat tower and, after adding two further stages, each distinguished by its lines of windows and ornamented walls, the spire was built under the direction of Richard of Farleigh, the master mason employed by Bishop Wyvil. Its weight, estimated at 6,400 tons, rests on four main pillars, each six foot in diameter, and to help them take the load a stone vault was built across the foot of the tower above

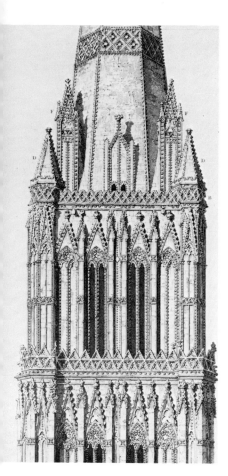

Salisbury Cathedral, the upper stage of the tower and the base of the spire. This detail, drawn in 1812, clearly shows the superb craftmanship of the medieval mason. Note how the pinnacles above the parapet of the tower hide the transition from square tower to octagonal spire.

the nave. A system of buttresses was built into the clerestory walls to break the outward thrust and a group of external flying buttresses inserted between the tower and aisle walls. Despite these precautions the stress caused the walls to shift and the four pillars to bend, (this can be clearly seen by looking upward from their base). The spire rises to 404 feet above ground level and Golding's novel brilliantly evokes the anxieties of men at work in a cathedral whose foundations – of gravel, rubble, brushwood and mud, were not designed to take the additional weight. The mood of *The Spire*, the pilgrims grouped round the west door 'listening for the threat and marvel of the singing pillars', the constant, almost obsessional, fear that the four columns might 'open apart like a flower, and everything else . . ., stone, wood, iron, glass, men, would slide down into the church like the fall of a mountain', must have haunted the cathedral during the thirty years that the spire took to complete. The builders braced the spire with iron bands and a century later two stone girder-arches were placed at the entrance to the main transepts between the supporting pillars. By then the cathedral's south-western foundations had already shifted, and when Sir Christopher Wren surveyed the building in 1668 he discovered that the spire leant $29\frac{1}{2}$ inches to the south-west. The cathedral was next examined in 1737. The lean had not increased and a brass plaque was set into the nave floor to mark the spot where the plumb-line fell.

The spire is the tallest in England, the second highest in Europe, and ever since its completion both cathedral and spire have received their share of criticism and praise. The nineteenth century antiquarian, John Britton, described the spire as an 'object of popular and scientific curiosity' and compared it to a maypole. William Beckford, the eccentric eighteenth century owner of the ill-fated Fonthill Abbey fifteen miles west of Salisbury, thought the cathedral 'poor, bare and insipid. All these windows, all this light, all this glass with its small diamond-shaped panes make this shameless church look like a whore clad only in muslin.' Beckford's distaste for light contradicts what Sir Arthur Bryant has justly called 'the crying need of the cloudy north.'

In purely visual terms the spire provides the long mass of choir and nave with the balance and proportion that it would otherwise lack. It has always exercised an almost magnetic fascination for the isolated communities on Salisbury Plain. 'We may discern', wrote John Aubrey when sixteen miles from the city, 'our Lady Church steeple at Sarum like a fine Spanish needle'. Easily visible above the high ground that circles the city, soaring upwards over the Close and surrounding streets, its aerial stillness provides a perfect contrast to the rolling undulations of chalk and pasture that are the essential features of the South Wiltshire downs.

'Let us descend joyfully to the plains, where the valleys abound in corn, where the fields are beautiful, and where there is freedom from oppression.' So wrote one of the canons before the decision to abandon Old Sarum. Such

The North Canonry. Though the present building dates from the late fifteenth century it was built over a large thirteenth century undercroft, contemporary no doubt with the cathedral.

sentiments were shared by others of the clergy, some of whom were perhaps more concerned with their physical well-being than the undoubted attractions of the meadows at Myrfield where the new cathedral was to be built. Their cramped and uncomfortable quarters on Old Sarum had little to commend them, and the laying out of the houses in what is still the largest Close in England took place at the same time as the construction of the cathedral. Soon after the move the chapter ordered the canons to build 'fair houses of stone' at their own expense and to begin work before a certain date or have their sites confiscated. The results of these demands are still visible. With its cathedral in the centre, Bishop's Palace to the south east, and canons' houses ranged along the North and West Walks, the Close is still characterized by that curious blend of space and seclusion that makes it the most beautiful in England.

Each of the houses in the West Walk offered ample proof of the wealth of its resident. They all had their own plots of land running down to the river and in 1402 the South Canonry (now the home of the bishop) contained a private chapel, bakery, brewhouse, stables and dovecote. Each of the houses had a great hall at its heart, and, although they have all been modified to suit changing needs, their medieval origins are still apparent. The trussed

27

rafter roof in the Old Deanery, directly opposite the west front of the cathedral and now part of the College of Sarum St. Michael, still survives, as does the ventilating turret which once acted as a chimney to the central hearth in the great hall. Other houses in the West Walk, amongst them the King's House (once the prebendal mansion of the abbots of Sherborne), the North Canonry, the Wardrobe (once the bishop's storehouse) and Hemingsby, can all be traced to the thirteenth century. Tudor, Jacobean, Georgian and Victorian additions have all left their mark on their interiors and façades, and the result is a delightful mixture of building materials and styles that does little to disturb the Close's unity.

Interdispersed amongst the grander houses were smaller residences for the vicars, chantry chaplains and other members of Minor Orders. The choristers and glazier once lived in Bishop's Walk and the vicars choral occupied their own Community House near St. Ann's Gate. The Bishop's Palace is set in its own grounds, and since 1947 has been the home of the Cathedral School. Only the vaulted undercroft survives intact from the palace built for Bishop Poore and its most striking feature is a late fifteenth century tower. The obvious delicacy of the cathedral spire and the risk of vibration weakening its walls meant that a separate belfry had to be built outside the cathedral. It was situated seventy yards north of the cathedral with walls eight feet thick, a 200 foot spire and a peal of ten bells. Even today, nearly two centuries after its inexcusable destruction by James Wyatt, the outline of its foundations can still be traced in the Close lawns.

On the southern rim of the Close was the College of St. Nicholas de Vaux founded by Bishop Giles de Bridport in 1261 as a university college attached to Oxford. One of the many unanswerable questions related to Salisbury's history is why it never became a university city in its own right. But, nevertheless, the foundation of de Vaux College marks the beginning of an academic tradition in the city that still persists. It was founded at a moment when student life in Oxford had been interrupted by the plague and was intended for 'poor, needy, well-born and teachable scholars'. Just inside the liberty of the Close stands St. Nicholas's Hospital, founded by Bishop Poore in the early thirteenth century. Originally a semi-religious community for 'receiving and supporting the poor', it has since evolved into a residential almshouse. A fifteenth century bishop ordered its inmates to be provided with wood and coal and the services of a barber and washerwoman and, in 1610, a master and chaplain were appointed to look after the welfare of 'six, poor, infirm persons' of either sex. Married couples were at first admitted but the behaviour of a Nicholas Newton and his wife, who 'brawled at board and threw bones before all the company', brought this privilege to an immediate halt. The Hospital is still an almshouse today, but only the two chapels at either end of the infirmary hall remain from the original buildings.

The boundaries of the Close were originally defined by the Avon to the west and south and a wide water-carrying ditch that left the river near Crane Bridge, skirted the north and east sides of the Close, and rejoined the Avon

Salisbury Cathedral, an eighteenth century engraving of the medieval belfry. The 200 foot spire was pulled down in 1768 and the remainder of the belfry, which once stood on the northern edge of the Close lawns, was demolished by James Wyatt circa 1789.

OPPOSITE ABOVE
The Bishop's Palace. Only the vaulted undercroft survives intact from the palace built by Bishop Poore. The tower was added in the late fifteenth century.

OPPOSITE BELOW
The south wing of the College of St. Nicholas de Vaux. founded by Bishop Bridport in 1261. The group of houses now occupying the site incorporate part of the medieval building.

29

St. Ann's Gate in the nineteenth century. From *Picturesque Memorials of Salisbury*, Peter Hall, 1834.

The south side of the Close Gate, the entrance into the High Street, from a nineteenth century engraving.

below Harnham Bridge. In 1327 the bishop was given a licence to strengthen the ditch with a crenellated wall and four years later he obtained permission to incorporate the remnants of the cathedral at Old Sarum (much of the Norman carving on the masonry is still visible). The wall runs along three sides of the Close and on its east side are Bishop's Gate and St. Ann's Gate (over whose archway there was once a chapel). Of the two remaining gates, Harnham Gate is the most southerly entrance into the Close and the High Street Gate leads directly into the city centre. The latter once had its own portcullis, a measure of the conflict between clergy and citizens that punctuated much of Salisbury's early history, and just outside the gate were the Close prison and porter's lodgings.

The construction of the cathedral and houses in the Close, the foundation of colleges, hospitals and almshouses, turned Salisbury into a major religious centre almost from the moment of its conception. Like moths to a flame, prelates, beggars, barons, scholars, kings, peasants and the infirm, flocked to the city from all over England. The canonization of St. Osmund increased the flow of pilgrims come to pray before his jewel-encrusted shrine in the cathedral. But although the building of the cathedral guaranteed Salisbury's existence, it owes its growth to an equally remarkable achievement – the foundation of the new city.

30

THREE

The New City

There be many fair streates in the City Saresbyri ... Al the streates, in a maner, in New Saresbyri, hath little streamlettes and arms derivyd out of Avon that runneth through them. The site of the very town of Saresbyri and much ground thereabout is playne and low, and is a pan or receyvor of most parts of the waters of Wiltshire.

JOHN LELAND *The Itinerary of John Leland*, 1534–1543

A traveller entering Salisbury from the west in the early fifteenth century had a choice of two approaches into the city. The older route, the ancient track that linked Wilton with Winchester, ran alongside the River Nadder before passing open fields where the townspeople cultivated strips of corn or grazed sheep and cattle in the common pasture. For the boundary between town and country was still indistinct. The surrounding farmland and placid river that wound round the edge of the city were a constant reminder of the countryside's proximity. A large proportion of the population were recent settlers who had come to Salisbury to seek a fortune within its ramparts. Those who forced a way through the monopolistic restrictions by which the burghers protected their own interests, who became mayors, aldermen and wealthy merchants, bought farms in the neighbouring villages and planted fruit trees and herbs in their city gardens. By law, all journeymen and apprentices were obliged to help gather in the harvest; meadows, piggeries and cowstalls could still be found in the city centre.

Once within sight of the cathedral the road passed through Fisherton Anger, 'a village . . . or ever New Saresbyri was builded', whose mill has survived, but whose dovecote, hop garden, withy beds and water meadows have all but vanished beneath the march of the suburbs. Taverns and cookhouses crowded the long approach to Fisherton Bridge. Above the din of the traffic the bells of the cathedral, two friaries and three parish churches could be heard calling the faithful to prayer. The road – rutted in summer, a quagmire in winter – would have been filled with pilgrims, craftsmen selling their wares from open doorways, peasants and yeomen returning to their homes after market, and carts and pack-horses laden with the canvas wrapped bales of raw wool that had brought Salisbury its wealth. Before paying a toll to a porter and crossing the six-arched stone bridge, then partly occupied by a skinner's shop and under repair 'for the easement of poor people with carts at flood time', the traveller passed the Dominican friary,

St. Edmund's Church. The collegiate church of St. Edmund of Abingdon (Edmund Rich had been Treasurer of Salisbury Cathedral during its construction) was founded by Bishop de la Wyle in 1269 to serve the newly created parish of St. Edmund. The existing tower was built during the Commonwealth to replace an earlier tower which fell in 1653. The church has recently been made redundant and is now in use as an Arts Centre.

Looking west along the River Avon towards Ayleswade Bridge. St. John's Chapel is on the central island and the Hospital of St. Nicholas on the right.

An enlargement of the central section of William Naish's map of Salisbury (1751 edition). Note the inclusion of the street channels.

built soon after the arrival of the Black Friars from Wilton in 1281. Above the bridge was a mill, built by Bishop Poore, where the city bakers ground their corn and part of whose income paid for the celebration of an annual cathedral mass. Below the bridge were a set of steps where the butchers cleaned carcasses and discarded unwanted offal, a practice that was eventually forbidden 'except it be in the current or shower of the river'.

The second western entrance into the city lay to the south of the Close, through the village of Harnham and over Ayleswade Bridge. The bridge had been built by Bishop Bingham in 1244 to provide additional revenue from tolls. By offering a more direct route into the West Country and by diverting traffic away from Wilton and Old Sarum it accelerated their decline and added to Salisbury's importance as a trading centre. To prevent the risk of flooding Bingham's engineers cut a second channel, forming an artificial island under one pier of the new bridge. A small chapel, dedicated to St. John the Baptist, was built on the island and the Hospital of St. Nicholas was charged with responsibility for the maintenance of both bridge and chapel. The bridge's condition gradually deteriorated and in 1413 the hospital was given permission to levy an additional toll on all goods crossing the bridge to help pay for its upkeep. Today the bridge is only used by local traffic and the chapel is a private house.

Once inside the city an observant stranger would have quickly noticed the difference between Salisbury and any other English city of a comparable size. Because Salisbury did not evolve out of a village, but was founded, from the outset, as an entire city with defined limits, its wide streets bore little similarity to the passageways and alleys that filled most medieval towns. The scale and size of its conception reflect Bishop Poore's determination to

32

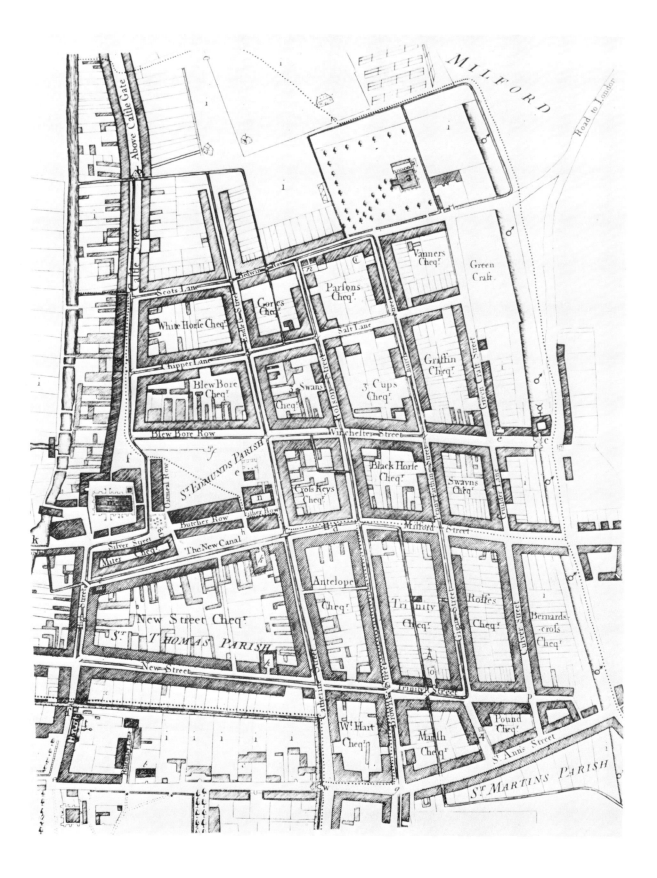

MILFORD

Road to London

Above Castle Gate

Castle Street

Scots Lane

White Horse Cheqr

Gores Cheqr

Parsons Cheqr.

Vanners Cheqr

Green Craft

Salt Lane

Chipper Lane

Blew Bore Cheqr

3 Swans Cheqr

3 Cups Cheqr

Griffin Cheqr

Green Craft Street

Blew Bore Row

Winchester Street

ST EDMUNDS PARISH

Oatmeal Row

Black Horse Cheqr

Crols Keys Cheqr

Swauns Cheqr

Butcher Row

Silver Street

Myter Cheqr

The New Canal

Milford Street

High Street

Antelope Cheqr

New Street Cheqr

Trinity Cheqr

Rolfes Cheqr

Bernards-crols Cheqr

St THOMAS PARISH

Catherine Street

Gigant Street

Culver Street

New Street

Wt Hart Cheqr

Maidh Cheqr

Pound Cheqr

St Anns Street

Trinity Street

ST MARTINS PARISH

found a well-watered city, with ample room for commerce and expansion, and with none of the disadvantages that characterized life on Old Sarum. The city was laid out at the same time as the cathedral and the streets were planned as a rectangular grid, five running parallel from north to south and six from east to west. They contained over twenty squares, or chequers, and it was around the rim of these squares that the first settlers built their houses. At the junction of the High Street and New Street is Mitre Corner, said to be the site of the first house built in the city and occupied by Poore whilst the Bishop's Palace and cathedral were being built. Since 1451 the bishop has always robed here before his enthronement, after which he is led into the cathedral by the dean and chapter in procession. The chequers took their names from either a tavern or wealthy resident; thus, a rich wool merchant gave his name to Swayne's Chequer and Blue Boar Row is all that survives of Blew Bore Chequer. Salisbury's design can be seen on an early city map and, even today, the remaining sections of the Chequers and the original street pattern are still clearly visible.

Through the streets of this bold experiment in medieval urban planning ran two systems of canals and street channels. Together they gave Salisbury its reputation for being an English Venice, but their 600 year existence now only survives in the name New Canal. They were probably intended as drainage ditches (for much of the city lies on marsh), but by 1875 when the last was filled in they were merely refuse-clogged open sewers that added little to the city's beauty. The more extensive of the two systems left the Avon through hatches to the west of Castle Street and criss-crossed the city. The other, a deeper, single channel known either as the Canal, Ditch or Common Trench, left the Avon below Fisherton Bridge, ran along New Canal and Milford Street, and then turned south to rejoin the Avon below Bugmore Meadows. The two systems ran at different levels and where they met small aqueducts carried the street channels over the Ditch. Both had bridges for pedestrians but an increase in the use of heavy waggons led to the demolition of the bridges, the widening of the channels, and the passing of a city ordinance ordering all wheeled traffic to travel along their cobbled beds. Their stench must have been abominable. The Canal was used as a dumping ground by the butchers and fishmongers in the market, the street channels were 'full of wet, filth and weeds, even in summer', and little was done to improve their condition until well into the eighteenth century.

From whichever direction one entered the city all roads led to the Market Place. Extending well beyond its present boundaries, as far south as New Canal and westward nearly to the river, it was a visible symbol of Salisbury's prestige. The licence to hold a market was first obtained even before the laying of the cathedral foundation stones (itself a significant comment on the priories of the founding fathers) and, in 1227, when the city was granted the royal charter that established it as a borough, the right to a weekly market and annual fair was re-affirmed. The market plots were a standard size, 16ft 6in wide and 38ft 6in deep, and the annual ground rent of 1/- was pay-

No. 1 Ox Row, a medieval timber-framed building, demolished in 1824.

able to the bishop. In 1361, after innumerable complaints from Wilton and Old Sarum that the market had become a daily event and a threat to their future prosperity, permission was given for a second weekly market. Since then Salisbury Market has always taken place on Tuesdays and Saturdays. The market was controlled by a bailiff on behalf of the bishop, and it was he who collected rents and handled applications for additional stalls. Its revenue was considerable, but the mayor and assembly were consistently thwarted in their attempts to obtain a share of its income. By the middle of the fifteenth century they had gained some control over its administration. They enforced the assize of ale and candles, maintained the city weighbeam, supervised the cleaning and paving of the Market Place and decided where the various commodities were to be sold.

Poultry Cross, first mentioned in 1335 as the site of the poultry and vegetable market, after its restoration in 1853.

The size of the Market Place has been much reduced since its foundation. Temporary stalls became permanent, some were replaced by shops and others became two or three storey houses with accommodation for the shopkeeper and his family. The process of encroachment was gradual, but several of the streets surrounding the Market Place were once passageways between lines of stalls. The medieval city contained four market crosses, near which certain goods were authorized to be sold. Poultry Cross, the site of the poultry, vegetable and fruit market, is the only survivor. The original cross was supposed to have been paid for as a penance by a fourteenth century knight who snatched a wafer from a priest in procession and ate it with an onion for his supper. The present cross dates from the fifteenth century. It was modernized in 1711 but restored in the medieval style in 1853. The Cheese Cross stood at the western end of the market near the site of the present library. The Wool Cross was in New Canal and Barnard's Cross, which marked the site of the first cattle market, stood on the southern side of the city near St. Ann Street. Names such as Fish Row, Cook's Row, Salt Lane, Ox Row, Oatmeal Row and Cordwainer Row are the only memorial to the countless tradesmen who once supplied the city with the raw materials on which its survival depended. Purveyors of charcoal, rope, yarn, hemp and straw were allotted sites to display their wares, whilst the 'abomination or filth' of livestock slaughter was confined to an open space behind Butcher Row. Hygiene regulations were unknown. Attempts by the city assembly to limit the melting of fat and disposal of offal in the Canal to the hours between sunset and sunrise were seldom obeyed. Ducks, pigs and geese scavenged through the streets. In October farmers from outlying villages brought their surplus cattle and pigs into Salisbury for slaughter. The meat was salted down into casks for winter consumption and the city tanners replenished their stocks of leather. Bread, bacon and ale formed the basis of the diet, but it was varied by fish and both resident and non-resident fishmongers had stalls on the south side of the Market Place. Herring from Ireland, oysters from Poole, sprats, hake and mackerel reached the city via Southampton or Bristol. In one year alone two merchants imported over 600 salmon.

Although the Market Place dominated Salisbury's commercial life, the city

Salisbury Market Place in about 1800, a drawing by Thomas Rowlandson. Note the two gentlemen in the stocks.

owed its prosperity to the wool and cloth trades. The thirteenth and fourteenth centuries were the 'great breeding season of English capitalism' and the export of wool, 'the sovereign merchandise and jewel of the realm', laid the foundations for its future wealth. The wool was collected, sampled, weighed and packed in staple towns, licensed to collect the tax levied by the crown on each sack intended for export. Salisbury is not mentioned on any surviving list of staple towns, but it had a Hall of the Staple in St. Martin's Church Street and quickly developed into an important regional centre for the marketing of raw wool. Vast flocks of sheep grazed the downland to its west and north, Southampton offered easy access to the textile towns of Flanders and Italy, and its merchants were quick to take advantage of their geographical good fortune. Men like Robert of Knoyle, John a'Port, William Swayne, John Hall and William Webb – truculent, independent, avaricious, turned Salisbury into one of the ten wealthiest cities in the country.

The growth of the cloth trade added to the city's reputation. The turning of raw wool into the best cloth called not for one craft but many – washing, carding, spinning, weaving, fulling and dyeing – and in combination they provided full employment for the labourers and artisans who lived in the medieval city. The looms were operated by men and once the cloth had been roughly woven it was beaten into shape by water powered hammers. The rhythmic shuttle of the loom and monotonous thump of the fulling mill must have been familiar sounds throughout the city. Vats, filled with brilliantly coloured dyes, occupied the narrow alleys that extended down to the

36

Avon to the west of Castle Street. In the Green Croft, on the east side of the city, the cloth was stretched and dried on racks before being baled. The striped cloth made in Salisbury was traditionally worn by the well-to-do peasant, but the overseas demand carried its merchants to Portugal and Bruges, into the Baltic and Mediterranean. A few had an interest in shipping, using their vessels to import dyes, wine and other foreign goods into the city. The Southampton Brokerage Books offer evidence of their flair for commerce. By early in the fifteenth century 25,000 gallons of wine a year passed through Salisbury. In 1451 one merchant imported garlic, onion seed, fish, madder, soap, teazles, hemp, tar, steel nails, tables, brushes, hats and tapestry covers. Most of these goods were stored in warehouses and then distributed to other towns in the south. John Hall owned his own shop, known as the 'Doggehole', and a caravel, the *James* of Poole. In 1463 its captain seized a French ship which, unfortunately for Hall, was carrying cloth under safe conduct from Edward IV. Such irritations were the price of success. For the city magnates flourished at a time when free enterprise and commercial ingenuity were breeding a new class of capitalist entrepreneur. They lent money, bought up wool stocks, and supplied craftsmen with the dyes and other materials needed for cloth. Owning barges, warehouses, tenements, shops and taverns, they exercised an influence over civic life quite out of proportion to their number. It was they who became mayor or represented the city in Parliament; they who turned Bishop Poore's vision of a bustling, energetic city into a reality. For

Castle Street looking south in the early nineteenth century. From John Britton's *Picturesque Antiquities of English Cities*.

Salisbury was perfectly tuned to the demands of the age. Spacious and accessible, it was one of the first cities in the country to realize that commerce and trade were shaping the future of English society.

Soon after the city's foundation its leading craftsmen formed a guild merchant to foster and protect their interests. It was soon well-established, and in 1249 a city craftsman, though born a villein and subject to feudal law, was able to retain his freedom by proving that he lived in Salisbury 'in scot and lot and in the guild merchant as a free burgess'. By 1306 it had over 300 members, admitted by either the bishop or mayor, on payment of a fee which was divided between them. As the city grew so did membership of the guild, and, by late in the fourteenth century, individual craft guilds had been formed to manage their own affairs, fix wages and prices and regulate conditions of work. The first surviving reference to a Salisbury craft guild concerns the skinners, but, by the mid-fifteenth century, thirty guilds existed in the city. Amongst them were those of the weavers, tailors, goldsmiths, brewers, barber-surgeons, pewterers and blacksmiths, and the complete list emphasizes the range of skills that flourished in the medieval city. By preventing strangers from trading in the city and by jealously guarding their rights, each guild was able to guarantee employment for its members and a market for their goods. When the skinners petitioned the tailors not to trespass on their rights 'by furring any garment for man or woman' they were re-stating the need for give-and-take between one guild and another. The guilds also fulfilled certain municipal obligations. In 1415 they supplied infantry and archers for the Agincourt campaign, and they were periodically asked to help dig the town ditch or repair the cobbled streets in the wards where their workshops were situated. The Salisbury craft guilds never gained much power. The supremacy of the bishop over the city institutions limited their responsibility and they were forbidden to form a guild merchant court.

The two largest guilds were those of the weavers and tailors. Both held land for the support of chantries in the city churches and both presented pageants on the eve of the city's patronal feast days. The Tailors' Guild owned the Giant, once known as St Christopher, who now lives in retirement in Salisbury Museum. Over twelve foot high, with a whiskery black face, he is the only English pageant giant to have survived into the twentieth century. On Midsummer's Eve the tailors went in procession to St John's Chapel on Ayleswade Bridge, afterwards returning to their hall near the Market Place where the regulations prescribed a 'drynkyng in the moste Godely wise'. The Giant went with them, accompanied by Hob-nob (his hobby horse), pages carrying his staff, sword and lantern, Morris dancers, three blackamoors and a devil. On the eve of the feast of St. George the mayor and assembly, dressed in scarlet and mounted on horseback, rode through the streets attended by minstrels, trumpeters and torchbearers. These celebrations, a grafting of pagan tradition and ancient custom on to Christian faith, stamped the city with its own special character. Isolation

The Salisbury Giant, with Hob-nob (his hobby horse), at the Coronation of George V in 1911.

38

St. Thomas's Church, Salisbury. The church was founded at the same time as the city as a chapel-of-ease for the builders of the cathedral to worship in. The present building dates from about 1470. Amongst its treasures are the Lady Chapel, built in 1470 by William Swayne as a chantry chapel for his family and the Tailors' Guild, and the Doom painting over the chancel arch.

knitted the community together. Bad roads and poor transport made it self-reliant and independent. Although most of the wealthier merchants were self-made men whose careers had begun in rural cottage or city tenement the talent and ambition that brought them success did not result in their leaving the city. Some gave money for street repairs, others left bequests towards the building of bars and gates. William Swayne founded a chantry in St. Thomas's Church and paid for the construction of the the south chapel. Instead of living in palatial manor houses on the outskirts of the city they built their homes close to its heart. John a'Port's timber framed house in Three Lyon Chequer was restored in the 1930s and is now a china shop. He was a man of 'evil disposition and great malice', but the deficiences in his character did not prevent him from being elected mayor six times. William Webb's house in Crane Street, although much altered in the nineteenth century, still possesses its stone archway and inner courtyard. But the most impressive of Salisbury's surviving medieval houses belonged to John Hall. Four times mayor of the city, arrogant and foul-mouthed, his stone house in New Canal abutted the Market Place on which his wealth depended. It was twice restored in the nineteenth century and was converted into a cinema foyer in the 1930s, but its timber roof and stone fireplace have been carefully preserved.

Men like Hall and Swayne were not typical of Salisbury's merchant class. The larger proportion of its population were poor, illiterate craftsmen who shared roof and board with their apprentices. The distinction between employer and employed was still in its infancy. Mutual respect and good-will were essential to the city's survival and the guild merchant and craft guilds echoed the need for unity. Dedicated to the principles of self-help, of no rights without duties, they encouraged civic pride and allowed Salisbury to develop its own identity and character.

In the late summer of 1348 Salisbury experienced a catastrophe that must have brought normal life to a standstill. It was a wet summer; sheep were struck down by disease and the harvest seemed certain to be poor. But the bad weather gave no indication of what lay ahead. In July the Black Death, carried into Europe during 1347 by Black Sea traders and already raging throughout the Continent, reached Normandy. In August it broke out along the Dorset coast. By September it had reached Salisbury on a journey that was only to end when it touched Scotland's northern shores. Princes, barons, priests and paupers; no one was immune. Few lived for more than three days once the inflamed lungs that marked its first symptoms gave way to its secondary stages. Although nothing is known about the precise effect of the plague on Salisbury we can be certain it exacted a heavy toll. The entire population of one nearby village perished. At the inquest of a Wiltshire land-owner killed by the plague it was discovered that his land was worthless and his tenants all dead. Such tales were commonplace throughout 1348 and 1349. Estimates suggest that nearly between a third and half the population of

The timber-roofed hall of John Hall's house in New Canal.

the British Isles died during the Black Death. There is no reason to assume that Salisbury's statistics were any different. The crowded tenements and unsanitary street channels were a natural breeding ground for the rat-flea that carried the disease. Open graves, carts collecting the dead, red crosses on doors, silent church bells, a deserted Market Place, a mood of pessimism and despair; such must have been the character of the city whilst the Black Death raged. And yet, incredible though it seems, even when the plague was at its height Richard of Farleigh and his masons carried on with the construction of a spire that is one of the crowning glories of English architecture.

The continuation of work on the spire during the Black Death was a rare and isolated example of the faith and zeal that had prompted the cathedral's foundation. Many believed that the plague was a divine punishment for human wickedness and vice. There was much to support this view, for there was a spiritual malaise in fourteenth century society that not even the Black Death could cure. No institution was more damned by its own shortcomings than the church itself. Its power was so great that it had lost contact with those to whom it preached. Its theology was too complex to be understood and its existence was dependent, not on prayer, but an army of financiers and ecclesiastical lawyers. The rewards of success were available in this world as much as the next. Many bishops led luxurious and indolent lives, canons were rarely in residence and the lower ranks in the church hierarchy were more eager to imitate their peers than attend to their duties. The moral decay of the medieval church was partly due to the pope's insistence on appointing foreigners, unable to speak English, to high office in the English church. Between 1297 and 1367 all six of Salisbury's deans were foreign relatives of the pope. Three of its precentors and four of its treasurers may never have set foot in the cathedral throughout their term of office. After 1330 all the fourteenth century bishops were civil servants.

Life inside Salisbury Close reflected the church's disunity and lack of purpose. The choristers had their own archery butts and the sexton ran a tavern in the belfry. Some of the vicars and chantry chaplains attended divine service accompanied by their hawks and dogs and the barking of the latter made prayer impossible. Many of the choristers failed to attend mass, and those that did often sang bawdy ballads instead of the solemn chants and psalms laid down in the order of service. The choristers were a perennial nuisance. To begin with they had lodged with various members of the chapter, but in the early fourteenth century Bishop Simon of Ghent gave them a house and the rent from a cellar in the fish shambles to help pay for their food, clothing and education. A warden, Alexander Hemingsby, was appointed to look after them, and their home, in the north-west corner of the Close, still bears his name. In the middle of the century they were moved into a house in Bishop's Walk, now known as the Choristers' House. This detailed attentiveness to their welfare had no effect on their behaviour. Rowdy and boisterous, often reprimanded for playing dice or knucklebones in the city, they were still forced 'to go round flocking to crave a beggar's pay . . . to get enough victuals to keep the wolf from the door'.

Clerical morals had little to commend them. Many of the vicars, and even the occasional canon, kept a mistress in the city. Although the cathedral statutes ordered the clergy to buy their bread from male bakers and forbade women to live in the Close lest 'aught that is unlawful be committed', nothing could prevent the vicars and chaplains from scaling the Close wall to keep appointments with the wives of Salisbury's citizens. The roll-call of ecclesiastical misdeamenours was endless. The vicars 'mocked God' by 'leaping and skipping' inside the cathedral. One was attacked by a fellow vicar with a dagger whilst returning home after matins. The statute against entertaining strangers was regularly abused. One visitor was murdered and his goods stolen, but the horde of 'Slanderers, Flatterers, Buffoons and Backbiters' whom the vicars liked to invite into their homes seem to have paid scant attention to the possibility of the crime being repeated. Clerical vanity was widespread. Some of the clergy wore high collars, hitched their gowns up round their knees and cut the hem into a fashionable fringe. Others affected pointed shoes with curled peaks, and those that did could neither kneel to pray nor walk upstairs unless they went up backwards.

Behaviour such as this was symptomatic of the state of church, both in Salisbury and throughout the country. Pardoners sold indulgences for remission of sins to the highest bidder, others made a living out of faking holy relics. Benefices were sold and pluralism was common. The power of the ecclesiastical courts, especially in Salisbury where the bishop was feudal over-lord, was arbitrary and absolute. Laymen were fined for failing to attend mass, for brawling or working on Sundays. Penances were often absurd or humiliating and the continual petty interference by the church in civilian life did not improve relations between the two quarters of the city.

Conflict between the bishop and city fathers was a permanent feature of life in medieval Salisbury. The relationship between the two soon soured, gradually developing into a clash of interests that involved argument, recrimination and occasional violence. Although Bishop Poore had been anxious to leave behind the irritations that had led to the evacuation of Old Sarum, the royal charter of 1227, which established the city as a borough, emphasized his superiority. The mayor had to be sworn into office either in his presence or that of his bailiff. This annual reminder of the bishop's supremacy soon became a source of dispute. The bailiffs delegated their duties to men without either 'substance or gravity' and the mayors, often Salisbury's wealthiest and most influential citizens, disliked having to defer to someone who was often no more than an ecclesiastical cipher. From the outset the bishop's powers were immense. He had the right to erect gallows and regulate the price of bread and ale, to enclose the city with ramparts, to alter the course of roads or bridges and, most controversial of all, to tax the city whenever the king taxed the royal demesnes.

But the charter of 1227 made some provision for the city's needs. Salisbury was declared a free city with freedom for its inhabitants from all tolls throughout England. They were permitted to elect a mayor, form an assembly and guild merchant, and all merchants were allowed to come and go as they wished, subject only to the legal tax on their goods. At first these arrangements suited the city. Protected by the bishop, assured of a percentage of the wealth attracted to the city by the cathedral, its citizens were content to establish the commercial reputation on which their future depended. Until that was done any attempt to gain their independence would be doomed to failure. By the end of the thirteenth century dispute was inevitable. The wool trade had turned the fledgling city into one of the most prosperous in the country. The bishop was determined to extract the maximum profit from his rights to rents, tolls and market income, and the mayor and assembly were eager to increase their share of the city's wealth.

In 1302, when Bishop Simon of Ghent ordered the city to be taxed, the rivalry between church and city broke out into the open. The mayor, assembly and guild merchant refused to pay the tax; partly because the demand lacked precedent and partly because it threatened their independence. Rather than submit to the right to future taxation they revoked the charter and surrendered their liberties. It was a hasty, ill-considered decision and the effect on trade was immediate. The townspeople were no longer exempt from the payment of tolls and, shorn of its borough status, the city was unable to safeguard the interests of its merchants and craftsmen. The assembly had badly misjudged its power and in 1306 submitted to the bishop's right to taxation in return for a renewal of the charter. The bishop had won a decisive victory and the agreement that ended the dispute re-affirmed his supremacy over every aspect of city life. But the clash must have warned him that outside the Close lay a turbulent, ambitious city whose obedience could not always be guaranteed. Political realities, not aesthetics, led to the replacement of the Close ditch by its existing wall in 1331.

The discontent smouldered on throughout the fourteenth century. On one occasion the bishop's bailiff was attacked when he was presiding over the bishop's court and its business was disrupted. On another a general pardon was granted to the citizens who, 'in no small number', had risen in revolt against the justices of the peace and formed illegal assemblies.

The early fifteenth century marked a revival of religious life in Salisbury. Bishop Hallam's sermons, his administrative skill and spiritual leadership, re-established the cathedral's reputation and its chapter gradually developed into one of the most distinguished ecclesiastical bodies of the late Middle Ages. Canons were replaced and persuaded to take up residence in the Close, a survey was made of the cathedral's property, inventories were ordered, statutes revised and the furniture and ornaments inspected. The change is best illustrated by the construction of the cathedral library above the east walk of the cloisters. Although Bishop Osmund's manuscripts formed the nucleus of the collection the library was rapidly enlarged and in due course became an important centre for scholastic and theological research. The Earl of Salisbury's copy of Magna Carta and the liturgical works connected to the performance of the Sarum Rite are the library's most remarkable legacy, but amongst the manuscripts are two tenth century Gallican psalters and a page from an eighth century Old Testament. Other rarities include the only surviving copy of *Fons Jacobi*, a fifteenth century devotional book, as well as a unique fourteenth century illuminated Tonale with the music shown in full, a fifteenth century Processionale and an illuminated Breviary. Amongst the books are thirty that pre-date 1500, including Caxton's *Golden Legend*.

But Salisbury's spiritual renaissance did not abolish all evidence of clerical chicanery and corruption. One member of the vicars choral acquired a mistress in the city and a reputation for profanity that made a nonsense of his religious vows. His behaviour became so outrageous that a deputation, led by the mayor, petitioned the dean for his imprisonment. Another cleric admitted to adultery with three women, quarrelled with his fellow vicars and was eventually tried for heresy. In 1454, when Richard Southsex went to collect the rent from the bishop's city tenants, he ran amuck through their gardens, killing poultry and geese with a sword. Justified complaints that he was a 'mad man and not of a sound mind' did not prevent him from ending his career as Sub-Magister of the Choristers. Incidents such as these need to be placed in their proper perspective, for there were many examples of clerical kindness that did much to ease the hardship of city life. Members of the chapter left money to be distributed amongst the sick and poor and one vicar gave 6d to each prisoner in the Guildhall.

The fifteenth century marked the summit of Salisbury's fortunes, but the mood of rebellion that had led to the events of 1306 was never far from the surface. In 1450, during Jack Cade's abortive peasant uprising, Bishop Ayscough exercised his right to tax the city. On this occasion the demand led to violence. A city mob, led by a brewer and butcher, besieged the bishop in his palace and forced him to flee to the Priory of Edington, on the north-west edge of Salisbury Plain. The mob followed, dragged the bishop from the altar and stoned him to death on a hill outside the priory. Ayscough was Henry VI's confessor and the link between his murder and Cade's rebellion was too much of a coincidence to be accidental. The murderers were hung and part of Cade's body was exhibited in the Market Place as a warning to the city to be wary of sedition.

Bishop Ayscough's murder was followed by a dispute, which although trivial, re-awoke the traditional antagonism between the church and city burghers. In 1465 William Swayne obtained permission from the bishop, Richard Beauchamp, to build a house for a chantry priest on a plot of land in St. Thomas's churchyard. The mayor, John Hall, insisted that the land belonged to the city and had the house demolished. Both sides petitioned Edward IV for support; the bishop accused Hall of constantly defying his authority and the city demanded complete control over its own affairs in return for an annual rent. Hall's arrogance did little to help Salisbury's cause. His 'seditious, hasty and unwitting disposition' led to his imprisonment and the assembly was ordered to elect a new mayor – of 'sad, sober and discreet disposition'. This they refused to do and a small delegation was appointed to present the assembly's case. The argument took nine years to resolve and once again ended in complete triumph for the bishop. Its outcome proves that between 1306 and 1474, during which years the city's wealth and prestige were at their height, it failed to find the political muscle to turn its wish for independence into a reality.

The main protagonists in the case, Hall and Swayne, dominated fifteenth century municipal life and their few recorded encounters leave no doubt as to their mutual dislike. 'I defy thou. What are thou? I am as rich as thou, knave, harlot.' 'I am of better birth than thou, and have born the worship and estate of this city and kept it as well as thou.' And so on, until the assembly was obliged to introduce a fine against invective if normal business was to continue. Hall was undoubtedly a remarkable man. After his release from prison he was re-elected mayor, and it was he who welcomed Edward IV into Salisbury when he next visited the city. But personal triumphs do not make permanent victories, and Hall had neither the talent or temper to outmanoeuvre the bishop in the protracted struggle for control of the city revenue. Had he done so Salisbury's medieval history might have been very different.

John Hall or Halle, died 1479, four times mayor of Salisbury and one of its wealthiest merchants.

The High Street facade of the Old George Inn in the late nineteenth century.

In 1377 Salisbury's population was estimated at 4,800, by 1527 it had only reached 6,000. Occasional outbreaks of plague and the high infant mortality rate kept it in check and a small hospital in Trinity Street was the sole refuge for the sick. Trinity Hospital was founded in 1379 as an act of penance by Agnes of Bottenham, an ex-innkeeper and brothel owner. It initially provided refuge for twelve 'poor persons' and daily board and lodging for twelve 'poor strangers'. By 1400 it had thirty beds and a contemporary chronicler described it as a place where 'the hungry were fed, the thirsty had drink, the naked were clothed, the sick were comforted, the dead were buried, the mad were restored to their reason, orphans and widows were nourished and lying-in women were cared for'. The hospital was rebuilt in the eighteenth century and is now a city almshouse.

Just off St. Ann Street, but also on the southern side of the city, stood the Franciscan Friary, founded in 1225 on land given to the Order by Bishop Poore only a year after a band of penniless, barefoot and bare-headed friars had landed at Dover. The impact of the Francisans on city life was immense. They led austere lives, wore coarse, grey gowns with rope girdles, and lived on barley bread and beer so bitter it had to be diluted to be drinkable. Their diocese was the city itself and their congregation its lepers, outcasts and beggars. In Salisbury they preached beneath the market crosses and ministered to the huddled masses in the city slums. For disease, poverty and overcrowding were widespread, and many of the poorer artisans lived in rough, one-room clay and wattle hovels whose rush floors were only changed once a year. Vice, felony, drunkenness and violence were common. The present High Street had at least six inns, amongst them the George, partly built with timbers from Old Sarum, which by early in the fifteenth century included shops, cellars, laundry houses, chambers and an inner courtyard where travelling players entertained their audience to juggling and miracle plays. The brothels were in Culver Street, but in 1452 their inmates were forced to leave the city for not wearing the striped hoods that were the symbol of their profession. At the eastern end of the Market Place stood the gallows, pillory and whipping post. Nearby were the stocks where brawlers and drunkards were pelted with filth and rotten fruit. In Milford Street, overlooking the foul waters of the Canal, was a ducking stool for the punishment of scolds and scandal-mongers.

Responsibility for the maintenance of law and order was divided between the bishop and assembly. The bishop's prison was in the Guildhall and a fortnightly court, presided over by his bailiff, dealt with all civil actions and administered the transfer of tenements and market plots. The monthly shire court had responsibility for small debts, trespass, affrays and public nuisance, whilst more serious criminal matters were transferred to the king's courts.

The first mayor had been elected soon after the foundation of the city and by the end of the thirteenth century a number of lesser officials had also been appointed. The assembly met in the Council House (which then stood between the Cheese Market and St. Thomas's Church), and by the mid-

Old George Yard in 1813.

Old George Yard, now a shopping precinct and renamed Old George Mall, as it is today.

fifteenth century it had evolved into two groups who between them shared out the duties of municipal government. There were four aldermen, one to each ward; two reeves, who collected rents and had the right to seize goods to enforce payment; two sergeants to superintend the prison; a city clerk; a watchman who apprehended vagrants; a beadle who rounded up stray animals; a sergeant-at-law who supervised repairs to city property; two chamberlains who collected and spent the city's income; constables; coroners and three minstrels whose livery and board were paid for by the city. The assembly took time to establish its authority, for all decisions had to be ratified by the bishop, but by the end of the fifteenth century it had assumed responsibility for the day-to-day administration of the city. Its members fixed the hour for bells to be rung to open and close the market, supervised repairs to bridges, ordered streets to be cleaned, controlled the removal of refuse from the Market Place, nominated Parliamentary representatives, paid a carter to collect dung and ordered the manning of bridges, gates and the city ramparts during times of national emergency.

The building of the ramparts and digging of the town ditch had first been started when the city was founded, and in 1367 Bishop Wyvil gave permission for the construction of four gates, a stone wall with turrets and an outer ditch. Progress was slow, the wall was never built, and the ramparts and ditch were not completed until well into the fifteenth century. They originally extended along the north and east sides of the city, but the ditch has since been filled in and only a short section of the ramparts still survive. The two most important gates were in Winchester Street and Castle Street. In the open meadows beyond the Castle Street Gate were the archery butts where the apprentice lads attended compulsory archery practice after church on Sundays.

The city gates were in constant use. After crossing the inhospitable downland that surrounded Salisbury and isolated it from the rest of the country the city taverns and pot-shops must have been a welcome sight to the pilgrims and merchants whose piety and acquisitiveness had led them to Salisbury. Others also were attracted to the city. Near Old Sarum, in a hollow in the downs, was one of England's five licensed tournament fields. Here, on the vivid green pasture that is the hallmark of the folded sheep, immense crowds witnessed the elaborate rituals of courtship and chivalry that accompanied the jousting. These crowds, though they filled the inns and spent freely at the market, were often unruly. Again and again they broke into and plundered the homes of the merchants and clergy. When Edward I ordered a tournament to be held in 1307 he was compelled to issue a letter forbidding any attack upon the houses in the Close.

The relationship between the crown and cathedral added to Salisbury's importance. The Confraternity of Salisbury Cathedral, founded to safeguard the cathedral's interests, included John of Gaunt, Henry IV and Joan, wife of Henry VI, amongst its members. The proximity of the royal hunting palace at Clarendon (the site is now overgrown) led to regular visits by the royal family and the barons and peers who filled the offices of state. Henry V attended the enthronement of Bishop Chandler in 1417; as two years earlier he had camped on Bishop Down before embarking for France and victory at Agincourt.

The links between Salisbury and Clarendon often led to a sudden influx of soldiers when the king was in residence. The city population seem to have had little sympathy for the military and their meetings often ended in violence. During a brawl on Fisherton Bridge in 1414 between soldiers and citizens three men died. The municipal ledgers record payment to a Welsh minstrel for the loss of his hood whilst fighting on behalf of the city. But the townsfolk, for all their antipathy towards anyone who threatened their independence, were forced to play their part in the military campaigns of the Hundred Years War. They provided archers, infantry and horses, and, because the Avon was navigable to the Christchurch and the city technically a port, they built and manned a ship, *The Trout*, which was used in defence of the Kent coast.

The royal visits were celebrated with all the pomp and pageantry that the city could muster. When Henry VII visited the city all twenty-four ex-mayors, robed in scarlet, were waiting at the city gate to welcome him. The Salisbury Giant was led in procession through the streets and minstrels, mummers and wrestlers entertained the royal household. Armed men with clubs reinforced the city constables in an attempt to keep the peace and surveyors supervised the removal of rubbish from the streets,

The presence of the cathedral, the trading activities of its merchants and the city's relationship with the crown made Salisbury more cosmopolitan than its size suggests. But its personality was uniquely its own. The reed-lined Avon, stained madder or indigo where it flowed past the dye vats; the timber framed houses with their mullioned windows and steep gables; the grubby street channels running through the city centre; the soaring cathedral spire and withdrawn world within the Close; the Market Place filled with livestock and stalls, gave Salisbury a character whose last traces still survive. In under 300 years it had grown from nothing into one of the most prosperous cities in the country. Its merchants, the generations of nameless craftsmen who lived and died in tenement and cottage, and the priests who served in the cathedral were its authentic voice. For the enterprise and vigour of commerce, the native genius of English craftsmanship and the wealth and vision of the church shaped medieval society. But the atmosphere of medieval Salisbury is best illustrated by the annual election of the Boy Bishop on St. Nicholas Day. Then the choristers formed a mock chapter, elected their own bishop, and went in solemn procession through the cathedral, past the real bishop, his dean and chapter, whilst the choir chanted 'out of the mouths of babes and sucklings hast thou ordained strength' in accordance with the order of service laid down by the Sarum Rite. The ceremony, with its spirit of irreverence and mock humility, was soon to be abandoned and a new, less tolerant world ushered in.

FOUR

Reformation and Decay

This is our doctrine, that every soul of what calling soever he be
– be he monk, be he preacher, be he prophet, be he apostle –
ought to be subject to King and magistrates.

JOHN JEWEL Bishop of Salisbury, 1560–1571

When death drives, the Grave thrives,
Coachman, Runne thou away, never so fast
One stride of mine, cuts off the Nimblest haste.

Broadside on the Plague, 1630

In 1529 Henry VIII's Reformation Parliament began a seven year sitting.
When it rose the death knell of the Middle Ages had been sounded. The
king, angered by the pope's refusal to allow him to divorce Catherine of
Aragon and marry his pregnant mistress, Anne Boleyn, had set into motion
a chain of events that completely changed English society. The Reformation had begun, and it was to be carried through with all the dogmatism and
injustice that normally attends a social revolution. But the king's matri-
monial affairs were not its only cause. Although the church and monasteries
provided the nation with its lawyers, diplomats, statesmen, doctors, civil servants and teachers, neither institution enjoyed the respect of the laity. Out of
a total population of under three million some 30,000 were clerics of one
form or another. Many had rendered great service, but their rewards were
equally high, and the church's power had turned it into a bastion of privilege and wealth. The ascetic ideals that had led to the foundation of the
monasteries were no longer practised, and the alms given to the monks by
the poor subsidized a life of luxury and indolence. These abuses were neither
forgotten nor ignored and the finger of blame was being increasingly directed
towards Rome. The gradual rise of English nationalism had made the population less willing to suffer papal interference in their affairs. Dispute was
unavoidable, the *status quo* was not immune to change, and Henry VIII's
impatience with all who stood in his way was merely a human failing that
hastened the inevitable.

Between 1529 and the middle years of Elizabeth I's reign the Reformation
transformed religious life in Salisbury. Its impact was immediate and permanent. The greatest loss was to the cathedral itself. Relics, censers, candles

– anything that smacked of Romanism – were removed. The Sarum Rite was suppressed, the black scrollwork that decorated the walls of the nave was painted over and many of the statues on the west front were taken down and destroyed. Reformist zeal had no time to stop and count the cost. St. Osmund's shrine, with its jewelled reliquary containing his skull, was dismantled, the ornamental plate was sold and Bishop Jewel's aversion to the symbols of idolatry led to the tragic destruction of much of the stained glass. Long though the list sounds the cathedral escaped lightly, for the members of its chapter were all secular canons and its bishops were traditionally royal rather than papal servants.

Before the Reformation was over the election of the Boy Bishop had been forbidden, the chantries suppressed, the prebends dissolved and the friaries, grammar school and de Vaux College had all been closed. Of all the religious houses in the city only the Hospital of St. Nicholas was left alone. Few of the institutions that closed ever re-opened their doors. The Dominican Friary, together with its gardens, graveyard and fishery, was sold. The building was demolished and replaced by an inn and its site has since been occupied by a theatre, wheelwright's yard, skating rink and the Maundrel Hall.

Salisbury's Reformation bishops managed to keep pace with the changes in theology without betraying their consciences. But survival was a skilled art. For although Henry VIII had declared himself supreme head of an independent Church of England his religious views remained orthodox. Bishop Shaxton (1535-1539) was the only one to offend the crown; he was removed from office, imprisoned in the Tower of London and condemned to death for heresy. Under the Protector Somerset the crusade against Romanism and superstition grew more rapid. The eight divisions of the daily office were reduced to two (the now familiar matins and evensong), a new Order of Communion was introduced, all preaching from the pulpit was temporarily banned and, in 1549, Cranmer's English Prayer Book, one of the Reformation's most enduring achievements, was issued to every parish church. Liturgical measures such as these led to the wholesale destruction of anything that bore the taint of Catholic imagery or art. Superb illuminated manuscripts whose only fault lay in their lettering and decoration were sacrificed in the name of reform. Salisbury's cathedral library still contains 180 medieval manuscripts, but it seems probable that many more were burnt.

The worst excesses were yet to come. Bishop Salcot, alias Capon (1539-1557) held the see when Queen Mary's accession led to the return of Catholicism. Salcot's willingness to change doctrinal horses in midstream, almost overnight and without any loss of conscience, offers no more than a hint of the zealousness with which he embraced the Catholic faith. He was cunning, ruthless and avaricious, and used his power to benefit his own purse. 'A capon hath devoured all' was how Bishop Jewel described his predecessor's acquisition of cathedral property. Salcot's eagerness to appease the queen and retain his episcopacy sent many Protestant martyrs to the stake. Three itinerant minstrels, one of whom had jokingly denied the presence of Christ's Body and Blood in the sacrament of the Eucharist, were amongst those burnt in the Market Place. Salisbury's most celebrated martyrs were a farmer, mason and tailor who refused to accept the authority of the pope and were tried for heresy in Fisherton Anger Church. At the end of the hearing the farmer, John Maundrel, courageously declared his belief that 'wooden images were food to roast a shoulder of mutton, but evil to the Church'. Such sentiments hastened his own incineration. All three men, together with Alice Moberly, the wife of the tailor, were burnt at two stakes where they 'most constantly gave their bodies to the fire, and their souls to the Lord for testimony of His truth'.

By 1560, the date of John Jewel's enthronement, Elizabeth I's genius for compromise had made the stake obsolete. Although Jewel destroyed the cathedral stained glass he was cultured, hard-working and a dedicated Anglican. Whilst bishop he wrote his *Apology for the Church of England*, which Elizabeth ordered to be chained to the reading desk in every parish church. He also befriended and partly educated Richard Hooker, later a cathedral canon and the author of *Ecclesiastical Polity*, a work whose philosophy and eloquence make it one of the finest pieces of prose in the English language.

When Jewel first visited Salisbury the cathedral was in danger of collapse. In 1559 the spire had been struck by lightning and a 60 foot crack had appeared near the summit. 'This happened before I arrived in Salisbury', wrote the bishop to a friend, 'or it would have been attributed to my coming'. Jewel's first task was to investigate the state of the diocese, and his findings emphasize Salcot's incompetence. The muniments were being eaten by vermin, the canons' houses and Close wall were in partial ruin and the maintenance of the cathedral had been completly neglected. The decay of the cathedral was reflected in the behaviour of the clergy. Some were known to attend Communion only three times a year. The Archdeacon of Wiltshire, released from his vows of celibacy by the reform of the church, had made up for lost opportunity by marrying two wives. Six canons were dismissed for infamy, another was criticized for preaching unsound doctrine and yet another was imprisoned for practising magic.

Bishop Jewel did all he could to correct these abuses. Ill-health had little effect on his stamina, he rarely slept for more than four hours a day and whilst in office preached in every parish pulpit in the diocese. To save money for the cathedral's restoration he insisted that all the canons remain in residence and pay for the repair of their own houses. Many were now married and the Close gradually lost its celibate character. Wealthy citizens were permitted to take up residence, a few shops began trading and some of the old prebendal mansions were sold. Bishop Jewel also encouraged an interest in music that has since become an important part of the cathedral's heritage. A number of distinguished composers, organists and musicians served as lay-vicars in the early seventeenth century. Amongst them was the composer and organist John Farrant. Farrant's career at Salisbury came to an abrupt halt when he attempted to murder the dean in his study; failure and certain dismissal did not prevent him from returning to the cathedral to sing his part in the anthem.

John Jewel, Bishop of Salisbury (1560–1571). From John Britton's *The Beauties of England and Wales, Volume XV, Wiltshire* (1814).

The city did not escape the Reformation unscathed. The chantry guilds were suppressed, their wealth confiscated and the guild merchants' effigy of St. George was destroyed. But perhaps the most significant indication of the passing of the Middle Ages was the assembly's decision that the 'watch on St. Osmund's night be no longer observed or kept'. This ancient ceremony, when the members of the guild merchants dressed in 'the best manner that may be' and followed the mayor into the cathedral to keep silent vigil before the saint's shrine, had lost its purpose with the shrine's destruction.

The years following the Reformation marked a gradual decline in the importance of the cloth trade and unemployment and poverty became widespread. For three hundred years wool and cloth had dominated city life. But the decline, though temporarily halted, never lost momentum and by 1840 there was only one wool factory in the city. The closure of foreign ports during the sixteenth century wars with Spain was the initial cause of the depression and by 1596 only three Salisbury merchants were trading through Southampton. Other factors accelerated the decline. The Dissolution of the Monasteries had led to immense changes in rural society. As the patterns of land ownership changed the cloth trade expanded into other towns in Wiltshire, particularly those in the north of the county. Salisbury's monopoly of Wiltshire wool had ended and the London financiers who now controlled the marketing of cloth bought as willingly from the new towns as they did from provincial cities like Salisbury.

But the fault lay partly with the conservatism of the city's weavers and clothiers. Entrenched behind the guilds and trained from apprenticeship to make the brilliantly coloured striped cloth that had made the city wealthy many found it hard to adjust to the changes in fashion, and, when they did, it was often too late. Salisbury's traditional output lost popularity, and when its weavers began manufacturing undyed broadcloth for sale in London they had to compete in an open market over which they had no control. In the mid-seventeenth century medley and Spanish cloth became fashionable, but the city craftsmen carried on making broadcloth even after the demand had fallen. Salisbury's decline as a major trading centre meant the end of its overseas trading links; the merchant magnates disappeared, the income from imports ceased and its prosperity dwindled.

The economic depression led to inevitable hardship inside the city and in 1549 there was an unsuccessful uprising on Harnham Hill in protest against unemployment. The first city workhouse was founded in the early seventeenth century and in 1623 the corporation established a brewhouse in Rollestone Street to raise funds for poor relief. It was not a success. The brewers were bitterly opposed to the additional competition, only 18 of the city's 100 innkeepers bought its ale and its doors soon closed. Other measures intended to aid the poor proved more effective. Fines for drunkenness were used to buy food, and wheat was distributed in times of scarcity.

Yet the Reformation and hardship that followed worked to the city's advantage in its fight for independence from the church. For while the bishop and dean were busy re-establishing the cathedral's prestige the powers of

The Council House, built in 1580 and destroyed by fire after the mayor's inaugural banquet in 1780.

the assembly grew unchecked. By the mid-sixteenth century its influence was far greater than the charter allowed. It acquired at least some of the property confiscated from the church and with the cathedral's fortunes at a low ebb there was little the bishop could do to limit municipal ambition. The assembly bought the freehold of the Green Croft, which though they then let was still used as a place of execution and for the burial of plague victims. In 1562 a scavenger was appointed to clear the streets of 'mire, dirt, dust and soil' and the assembly issued instructions that all refuse heaps were to be kept free of stable dung and garden weeds. To reduce the risk of disease and fire over-crowding was penalized, the use of thatch banned and any infringement of the fire regulations punished by a payment of tar. To maintain the quality of the goods sold in the Market Place aletasters, sealers of leather and searchers of cloth and flesh were appointed.

The construction of a new Council House in 1580 provided the bishop with visible proof of the assembly's wealth and power. It was built at the eastern end of the Market Place and its timber framed two storeys, open colonnaded sides and squat domed tower symbolized the rising ambition of the city fathers. The establishment of an annual race meeting in open ground near Wilton five years later was additional evidence of the city's determination to extend its influence and attract wealth into the city. The Earl of Pembroke, owner of Wilton House, gave a gold bell worth £50, and Salisbury Races, which still continue, had begun their existence. By the middle of the seventeenth century a cup, scales and weights had been provided by the mayor, and citizens were appointed to act as starters and fire muskets at each of the mile posts.

The enmity between bishop and mayor, dormant since 1474, erupted for the final time in 1593 when a Royal Commission described the mayor as 'the bishop's mayor of his city of Salisbury. The obvious insinuation of ecclesiastical supremacy did not pass unnoticed and the next mayor refused to take his oath of office. Nearly twenty years of claim, counter-claim, petition and negotiation then followed before, almost an anti-climax after four centuries of dispute, James I suddenly granted the city the Charter of Incorporation that had eluded it for so long.

The Charter of 1612 incorporated Salisbury as a self-governing city under a mayor and corporation. The ancient boundaries of the city were confirmed and the jurisdiction of the bishop was limited to the liberty of the Close. The bishop was permitted to maintain a prison, pillory and stocks but his authority over the city ceased. From now on Salisbury's elected corporation were to be masters of the city's destiny, and though neither a particularly enlightened nor efficient body, they were to run the city until the corporation was remodelled in 1836.

To help win independence the assembly had argued that the division of power between mayor and bishop hindered effective government. The new corporation was determined to test its authority over the city and immediately ordered all the crafts and trades to form companies and submit constitutions for approval. The Salisbury trade companies were to dominate its commercial life for the next two centuries, but the regulations and restrictions with which they safeguarded their own interests were not designed to encourage expansion. No one who had not been apprenticed in the city was allowed to open up shop within its ramparts. Strangers were expelled, and those that stayed were taxed double if they owned or rented property in the city. Regulations such as these minimized competition and the new companies, unwieldy, bureaucratic and traditionalist, settled down to business in the certainty that they had no rivals.

The first company to be formed was the smiths and amongst its members were the saddlers, bell-founders, armourers, pin and cardmakers. The joiners' company included the bookbinders, millwrights, coopers, bellows-makers, painters, ropemakers, turners, instrument makers and freemasons, and the complete list of companies echoes the diversity of pre-industrial urban life. The Joiners' Hall in St. Ann Street still stands and its superb Jacobean façade and wood-mullioned windows mirror the high standards of craftsmanship that once flourished in the city. The regulations that governed the companies were often highly complex. The bakers were not allowed to sell bread in the market and, so as not to infringe the rights of the cooks, they were only permitted to bake cakes for funerals, Good Friday and at Christmas. The barber-surgeons forbade women to perform operations, 'for they do oftentimes take cures on them, to the great danger of the patient'. The barber-surgeons had the dubious privilege of being given the corpses of executed criminals for the study of anatomy.

During the early years of the seventeenth century Salisbury enjoyed a brief period of calm. Its independence was assured and although the sawing off of the supports to the mayor's seat in the cathedral may have irritated its incumbent and amused the choristers it did not disturb the city's tranquillity. The character of these years is captured in a memorial in the south aisle of the nave which shows a Tudor lady in high ruffed collar kneeling at prayer. The woman was Dame Elinor Sadler, 'so good a wife and grave a matron', who died aged eighty in 1623 and was 'interred under this pew, wherein with great devotion she had served God daily for almost 50 years'. Dame Elinor's second husband was Sir Thomas Sadler, owner of King's House, once the property of the Abbots of Sherborne, and it was here that James I stayed on his occasional visits to the city.

But the peace was to be short-lived, for two years after Dame Elinor's death the plague broke out in London. To prevent it reaching Salisbury goods and travellers from the capital were refused entry into the city. These measures delayed the inevitable but in 1627 the plague claimed its first Salisbury victims. The result was panic, and within four days there had been a partial evacuation of the city. Many abandoned their homes and fled into the country, and the city was left in the hands of about 3,000 impoverished artisans with nowhere else to go. The clergy blockaded themselves into the Close and

The Joiners' Hall in St. Ann Street, built in the Jacobean style in the early seventeenth century and now the property of the National Trust.

built platforms so that food could be passed over the wall. The only member of the corporation not to desert the city was its mayor, John Ivie. His chances of maintaining law and order seemed hopeless. The corporation funds stood at £80, looting had already begun, and his household consisted of one sergeant, two constables and two family retainers.

Many years later John Ivie wrote a vivid account of the events that took place in the plague-bound city. *The Declaration* was the work of a remarkable man. For Ivie's loyalty to Salisbury was unswerving and he used every tactic he could devise to keep its population under control. He built a granary in each of the three city parishes, persuaded a baker to return to his ovens and ordered the daily distribution of bread and beer. His hardest task was to find bearers willing to carry corpses to the city burial pits. The work

56

was unpleasant, no one was willing to offer them lodging and they faced certain persecution from the mobs that roamed the streets. Hot and cold water was thrown at them, nine died from the plague and they eventually armed themselves with sticks, went on strike and demanded a rise in their 4/- a week wage. The mayor was not easily intimidated. He hitched up his gown, 'look't about for stones in the street and put them into the skirt', called on support from passers-by and began stoning the unfortunate bearers. They quickly fled, taking refuge in a temporary shelter that had been built for them to sleep in. Ivie followed and after firing a few shots from a musket and agreeing to their demand for extra Bibles and shirts, he persuaded the bearers to return to work.

The mood in the beleaguered city ranged from recklessness and insobriety to one of complete despair. The rules of civilized behaviour were forgotten as the 'Drunkards, Whoremasters, and lewd fellows with all their allies' filled the ale-houses and taverns. Once, when touring the city, Ivie saw four bearers dancing round the graves in St. Thomas's churchyard with pots of ale on their shoulders chanting 'Hie for more shoulder-work'. A deranged widow set fire to the city pest-house and when Ivie arrived he found the pest-house destroyed and its thirty-seven inmates 'sitting in the field on the bare earth, in a miserable condition, many of them almost naked, and one of them quite naked'. The situation was rapidly worsening and Ivie ordered the city's 50 inns and 80 ale-houses to close their doors. Only one ale-house ignored his instructions. The landlord, his wife, maid and four weavers barricaded themselves in and drank their way through a tub of ale. Within three days they were all dead. There is just a hint of smugness in Ivie's description of their death: 'It pleased God to give me power to suppress all, saving that one house; and then the power of God did suppress that house in His own judgement'.

Nearly 400 people died in the plague. The figures for one parish are not known and the total would have been much higher if John Ivie had not stayed in the city. Almost single-handedly he fed it, maintained law and order and made certain that the corpses were cleared from the streets. His achievement has not been forgotten. The street where he is thought to have lived is now called Ivy Street and in 1932 a plaque was unveiled to his memory in the Guildhall.

Three years after the plague a new parson was inducted into the living of Bemerton, a small hamlet that borders the Nadder on the western outskirts of the city. His name was George Herbert, and it was here, in what is still one of the most unspoilt and peaceful areas of Salisbury, that, in the words of Lord David Cecil, the 'subtlest and most intimate of English religious poets' was to spend his final years. Herbert was a distant relative of the Earl of Pembroke and in early life had been a courtier. But the 'painted pleasures of Court life' soon palled; his wit was too quick, his brain 'a penknife in too narrow a sheaf' and his political ambitions had faded. He moved into the parsonage at Bemerton with his wife and two nieces and at once set about re-

One of the six timber corbels that line the facade of the Joiners' Hall, St. Ann Street.

57

The poet George Herbert (1593–1633).

pairing the church and farming the six acres of glebe that went with the living. The three years left to Herbert were to be amongst his most creative. It was at Bemerton that he wrote much of his poetry, including his version of Psalm 23, and in *A Country Parson* laid down the duties of the country clergyman. He began writing and composing hymns which he then sang to his wife, accompanied by either viol or lute. Twice a week he walked into Salisbury to listen to the singing in the cathedral, afterwards going to the house of some friends to play and make music. The poet was dedicated to his parish duties and his biographer, Isaak Walton, the son of the author of *The Compleat Angler*, states that 'some of the meaner sort did so love and reverence Mr Herbert that they would let their ploughs rest when Mr Herbert's Saints Bell rang to prayers': no small tribute in an age when, as John Aubrey commented, few farm workers had 'time to contemplate religion'.

George Herbert was already suffering from consumption on arrival at Bemerton and he died in 1633 at the age of thirty-nine. Before his death he wrote a short poem to his successor over the mantelpiece in the hall of the parsonage and its six lines have since been engraved onto the front wall of the house.

> If thou chance for to find
> a new house to thy mind
> and built without thy cost,
> Be good to the poor
> as God gives thee store
> and then thy labour's not lost.

In 1642 the Civil War started. From the outset Salisbury's sympathies, like those of most other cloth towns, lay firmly with Parliament. The political and religious discussion that preceded the war found easy nourishment amongst the city craftsmen and shopkeepers. The mayor was quick to rally support and a band of volunteers was soon formed. His attempt to forestall the Royalists by confiscating all arms and strengthening the ramparts proved ineffective, for after Edgehill the city was occupied by Prince Maurice for the king and the mayor was imprisoned in his own jail. But the lack of proper defences and the absence of a military garrison saved Salisbury from the worst excesses of war. It was never subjected to siege and played no part in any major campaign.

The city was first occupied by Parliamentary troops in the early summer of 1644. In June the Parliamentarian general, Edmund Ludlow, was pursued through the city after his defeat in a skirmish near Warminster. As 'divers persons disaffected to Parliament were so unwise as to display their pleasure' at the sight of the general being chased through the streets, he promptly returned to the city and fined all those with known Royalist sympathies. In September Charles I passed through the city at the head of an 11,000 strong army, and three months later the Royalist force left behind to garrison the city was attacked by a small detachment of Ludlow's men. The Roundheads burnt down the Close gates and took the Royalists prisoner. But the

Parliamentary triumph was to be short-lived. In January 1645, under cover of darkness, a party of Royalists entered the city through the Castle Street Gate. Ludlow counter-attacked. Followed by 30 troopers he broke out of the Close, crossed the Market Place and drove the Royalists up Endless Street. The street, despite its name, was a dead-end. The Royalists turned and forced Ludlow back into the Close. By dawn Ludlow had fled the city, leaving behind only a small garrison to defend the belfry. The fighting ended when the Royalists 'forced a collier to drive his cart loaden with charcoal to the door of the belfry (where he lost his life), and with it burnt down the door'. The behaviour of the Royalists during the occupation that followed did little to aid their cause. They committed 'such horrid outrages and barbarities' that they alienated the city and were eventually forced to leave.

Parliament's final victory gave the corporation a unique opportunity to undermine the bishop's authority. As Parliament had 'happily removed episcopacy' and the corporation, in their own words, had long been 'miserably enslaved' by the 'prelatical tyranny' of the bishop, they were given permission to purchase the bishop's lands, liberties and jurisdictions from the state. The Close clergy were expelled, their property was confiscated and four of the canons' houses were handed over to Puritan ministers – one of whom was appointed to the cathedral. The Bishop's Palace was converted into tenements, one becoming an inn kept by a tailor. The Close was used as a slaughter yard and communal rubbish dump and the constant turning of carts did serious damage to the graves. In 1653 Dutch prisoners were temporarily housed in the cathedral cloisters and library. But the generosity of various local gentry saved the cathedral from deterioration and throughout the Commonwealth craftsmen were secretly employed to maintain the stonework and roof.

The years that followed the Civil War show Salisbury at its worst. The city suffered from administrative neglect and when John Evelyn visited it he found the streets dirty, the water channels polluted and many of the buildings in a 'despicable' state. Puritan intolerance led to the persecution of anyone suspected of witchcraft or being a Quaker. One Quakeress was flogged for preaching, imprisoned in a windowless dungeon in the hope that she might recant, and only released when the mayor intervened. An eighty-year-old woman was executed at Fisherton gaol on suspicion that she could turn into a cat and another was executed for supposedly bewitching a young girl. Aubrey mentions the existence of a coven of eight Wiltshire witches who were all hung for 'flying in the air on a staff'.

These were improbable years, and although time has obscured much of what took place in Salisbury one incident hints at the anti-clerical feeling that existed in the city. In 1655 'old Halley', a plumber, roasted a leg of mutton and two chickens on top of 'Our Lady Spire'. Halley's culinary dexterity may have delighted his audience, but as an act of ridicule it symbolized the city's supremacy over a church that was without a bishop and whose future was uncertain.

FIVE

Restoration and Revival

The big provincial towns were like London but with less
wealth and more poverty, more despair, less social order, less
charity, more disease, but, like London, full of opportunity for
men of tough temperament, endless vigour, and resource to ac-
quire the modest affluence necessary to enter the demi-paradise
of comfort and ease which the eighteenth century afforded for
hard cash.

J. H. PLUMB *England in the Eighteenth Century*

In May 1660 Charles II returned to England from exile in France to claim his
father's throne; the Interregnum was over, the Restoration had begun. The
return of the monarchy had an immediate affect on life in Salisbury. The
Puritan ministers were evicted from the Close and a new bishop was enthroned. The charter granted by Cromwell was annulled, the Cap of Maintenance and Sword of State which he had presented to the city were taken to
the whipping post and destroyed, and the corporation was ordered to place
the king's arms over Castle Street Gate and the North Gate of the Close.

The Restoration was to mark the start of a cultural and spiritual renaissance in Salisbury that lasted until well into the eighteenth century and
whose legacy is still evident. Under Bishop Ward (1667-1689) the cathedral
gained a reputation for 'excellent Preaching, and Divine Service celebrated
with exemplary Piety, admirable Decency, and Celestial Music'. Few of Seth
Ward's successors had either his intelligence or influence, but none of them
prevented the cathedral from becoming a major force in English religious life.
As Salisbury's importance as a trading centre declined the patronage of the
cathedral became vital to its future prosperity. The conflict with the bishops
receded into the past and the city slowly shed the intense civic patriotism
that had tempered its medieval history. The prestige of the market rose
and the city gradually developed into a meeting place in which the local
gentry could shop, dance, exchange gossip and run the affairs of the county.
Many of them settled in the city, and only a brief visit to the Close is needed
to appreciate the architecture of the post-Restoration years. Modest affluence
and genteel respectability reshaped the city's character and by 1800 it had
acquired the air of provincial elegance it wears so well today.

But at the time of the Restoration the city's future was uncertain. Unemployment was high and the cloth trade was in recession. John Ivie, frail and

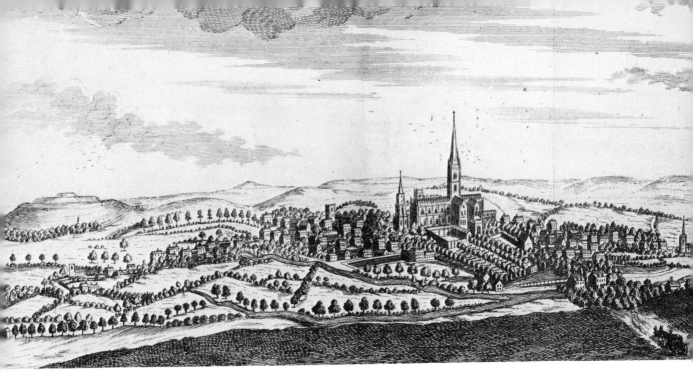

embittered but as outspoken as ever, was appalled at the inefficiency of the corporation and by the poverty that still existed in the city. 'Our beggars are so clamorous that they are like sometimes to pull travellers of any rank from their horses every morning, to the great scandal of our Government... Our poor do swarm about the City, Close and Country, and without restraint, whereby Bastardy is much increased, to the great grief of the inhabitants'. The corporation did little to remedy the situation and it was left to private philanthropy to ease the hardship of the poor. Gifts of food and clothing were distributed in the city slums, municipal charities were established and, within a century of the Restoration, an infirmary and six new almshouses had been built in the city. Amongst the almshouses, all of which still stand, were Margaret Blechynden's in Winchester Street, founded for six poor widows of 'good conversation and above the age of 50'; Sutton's in St. Ann Street, 'for three poor weavers and their widows after them'; and Frowd's in Bedwin Street, established to provide a home for twelve destitute bachelors and spinsters. But the most famous of the new almshouses was the College of Matrons, founded by Bishop Ward in 1682 in the Close for the widows of twelve clergymen who had been ordained in the dioceses of Salisbury or Exeter. The red brick building, which may have been designed by Sir Christopher Wren, was faced with the royal arms and each matron was given two rooms and a small garden. The rules that governed the college were carefully stated. Each matron was expected to attend divine service in the cathedral twice daily and none was to be absent from the Close for more than one month in the year. The bishop's motives for founding the college remain unclear. It has been suggested that he intended it to be a home for an impoverished clergyman's widow who, in her youth, had rejected his proposal of marriage; such anomalies only add to our interest in Bishop Ward.

A view of Salisbury from Harnham Hill in 1723.

61

The pediment of the Matrons'
College, founded in 1682 in the
Close by Seth Ward.

Seth Ward was one of the most remarkable men of his age. He was
created Bishop of Salisbury at the age of fifty in 1667 and for the next
twenty-two years dominated religious and cultural life in the city. He had
begun his career as a mathematician and astronomer and his research into
the orbital nature of planets made him a central figure in the scientific move-
ment of the late seventeenth century. As a founder member of the Royal
Society he numbered Charles II, Wren, Pepys and Isaac Newton amongst
his friends. He was shrewd, methodical and a devout Anglican. He was also
a hypochondriac. At the slightest suggestion of illness he would go for a
twenty mile gallop over the downs and, if fresh air and exercise failed to
effect a cure, he would resort to one of the many quack recipes which he
stored in a collection of notebooks. Amongst his remedies for gout was one

62

whose principal ingredients were a stuffed goose and a dead cat well-beaten with a rolling pin; a cure more likely to harm than soothe. According to his biographer he 'would take pills and potions when he had no need of them, from which not only I endeavoured to divert him, telling him that 'twas spending the ammunition before the town was besieged'. But no amount of good advice could prevent the bishop from concocting some new purge or specific. An imagined infection of the toe cost him over £200 (perhaps £2,000 in modern currency) 'in spirits of wine, in dry and wet baths, apothecaries and surgeons, who took his money and laughed at him in their sleeves'.

Seth Ward, Bishop of Salisbury (1667–1689).

Soon after his arrival in Salisbury Seth Ward ordered the Bishop's Palace to be rebuilt and the cathedral to be repaired. In 1669 he invited Christopher Wren to survey the cathedral and the manuscript notebook containing the architect's findings is still preserved in the cathedral library. The cathedral's proportions, the height of the nave and the lack of affectation, 'of filling every corner with ornaments, which glut the eye, as much as in Music too much division cloys the ear', delighted Wren, and he restricted his criticism to the state of the spire and the furnishings in the choir. Wren has also been associated with the building of the College of Matrons and Wren Hall, once the choristers' school-house in the north-west corner of the Close. But there is no evidence to suggest that he was ever consulted over either design, and it seems probable that his only major work in Salisbury was the supervision of the strengthening of the spire and the refurnishing of the choir.

Seth Ward's episcopacy initiated a cultural revival in Salisbury that embraced both art and science. The early death of the portrait painter John Greenhill robbed the city of an artist of perhaps major potential. Insobriety and dissipation were Greenhill's ruin – he drowned in a London ditch after leaving a brothel whilst drunk – but his portrait of Seth Ward, which still hangs in the Council House, hints at the breadth of his talent.

The cathedral organist Henry Wise was another victim of his own weaknesses. Argumentative, obstinate, prone to 'intemperate drinking and other excesses', he was killed in a scuffle in the Close after quarrelling with his wife and attacking a nightwatchman.

The eye-surgeon Dr. Tuberville was another late seventeenth century resident of the Close. Dr. Turberville's ingenious mixture of quackery, surgery and long-winded diagnosis made him one of the wealthiest men in the city. He was consulted by the royal family and Pepys, and patients from as far afield as Jamaica filled the city inns whilst undergoing treatment. Indeed, one visitor to Salisbury, who knew nothing of Tuberville, saw so many people with bandaged eyes that he assumed the population suffered from hereditary blindness. The doctor's cures ranged from blood-letting to the use of ointments, whilst his prescription for myopia meant shaving the head and smoking tobacco, 'which he had often known to do much good and never any harm to the eyes'.

The philosopher Thomas Chubb was born and educated in Salisbury. After briefly enjoying the patronage of literary London Chubb returned to his

The painter John Greenhill (1644?–1676). Greenhill was a pupil of Sir Peter Lely; a portrait of Charles II, attributed to Greenhill, hangs in the National Portrait Gallery.

The deist philosopher Thomas Chubb (1679–1747).

family gloving business and started writing a series of papers which pioneered discussion on rational thinking. He was later to influence both Voltaire and Coleridge, whilst Pope, writing to the poet John Gay, described him as 'a wonderful phenomenon of Wiltshire'.

Bishop Ward did much to reduce the traditional hostility between the clergy and the corporation, both by attracting wealth to the city and by his willingness to enter into its way of life. In 1672 he gave his support to a scheme to make the Avon navigable to Christchurch, an ambitious undertaking which had always previously failed for lack of funds. With Seth Ward's encouragement the money was raised, the river widened, locks built, and in 1684 two 25 ton wherries docked alongside Ayleswade Bridge.

The final years of Seth Ward's episcopacy were marred by a long and unpleasant quarrel with the dean, Dr. Pierce, which in time impaired the bishop's mind and led to sudden lapses of memory. The dean accused Ward of supporting Cromwell during the Interregnum, but, now it was over, of intolerance towards the many Nonconformists who still lived in the city. He launched his attack by publishing a satirical pamphlet intended to destroy Ward's reputation and the administration of the cathedral was largely ignored whilst its two leading dignitaries indulged their differences. Seth Ward never recovered from the viciousness of Pierce's attack, his health suffered, he retired to bed, and died a broken man. For the final month of his life he lived entirely on stock and by the date of his death was almost a skeleton. His superb collection of early scientific, mathematical and medical books is still preserved in the cathedral library, but his was a tragic end, for in just over twenty years he had done more to raise the prestige of the cathedral and city than had been achieved in the preceding two centuries.

In September 1668 Samuel Pepys arrived in Salisbury. He stayed in the Old George Inn and, after a 'good diet' and a night's rest between silk sheets, went to call on 'my friend Dr. Ward'. Pepys thought the 'tall-spired town' a 'very brave place', but the main purpose of his visit was an expedition to Stonehenge. Saddle horses and a guide were hired and Pepys's party began the eight mile ride out to the stones. A shepherd girl was paid 4d to lead the horses for the final part of the way. Once there Pepys was satisfied.

An imaginative but inaccurate engraving of the north east side of Stonehenge in the early eighteenth century. From William Stukeley's *Stonehenge* (1740).

64

An eighteenth century print of the parlour of 'The Barracks', a house in Brown Street.

The stones were 'as prodigious as any tales I ever heard, and worth going this journey to see: God knows what their use was! they are hard to tell, but yet may be told'. After returning to the city via Wilton Pepys spent the evening wandering amongst the tombs in the cathedral listening to the music from the choir. It was almost the perfect end to a perfect day. But the horses, beds and food all had to be paid for and the final bill was 'so exorbitant, and particular in rate of my horses, and 7s. 6d. for bread and beer that I was mad, and resolve to trouble the mistress about it and get something for the poor, and come away in that humour – £2 5s. 6d., servants 1s. 6d., poor 1s., guide to the stones 2s., poor woman in the street 1s., ribbons 9d., washwoman 1s. . . .' On the next day, to save money, he moved into a cheaper inn on the outskirts of the city, where the beds were 'good but lousy, which made us merry'.

Another contemporary visitor to Salisbury was Celia Fiennes, herself a native of Wiltshire and the author of *Through England on a Side Saddle in the Time of William and Mary*. Celia Fiennes admired the general design of the city and its broad streets, but gave scant praise to the 'little rivulets of water' which coursed down the middle of so many. For 'they maketh the streets not so clean or so easy to pass in, (although) they have steps to cross it and many open places for horses and carriages to cross it – it taketh off much from the beauty of the streets'. Celia Fiennes understated her case. For the streets, Market Place and Canal were still as filthy as ever, and the lack of sanitation was the cause of a succession of outbreaks of smallpox and a further attack of the plague in which 600 died.

Had both Pepys and Celia Fiennes waited until after the turn of the eighteenth century to record their impressions of Salisbury they would have found a changing city. For the Queen Anne and Georgian houses built by the gentry in the Close reflected the growing elegance of city life. Perhaps the most perfect of these new houses is Mompesson House, started in about 1680 by Thomas Mompesson, whose country seat was in the Wylye valley, and finished by his son in the reign of Queen Anne. Mompesson House, now owned by the National Trust, is typical of the eighteenth century

Mompesson House. The house, started by Thomas Mompesson in about 1680 and finished in the early seventeenth century, is now the property of the National Trust.

provincial town houses in which the local gentry spent part of each year; partly, I suspect, to dispose of their unmarried daughters. Its tall sash windows, perfectly proportioned rooms, wrought iron gates and lamp carriers, coat of arms emblazoned over the porch and original lead piping, are characteristic of the very best in early eighteenth century architecture. In the West Walk of the Close are both the Walton Canonry, rebuilt in 1719 after a fire and named after Isaak Walton, a cathedral canon and biographer of George Herbert; and Myles Place, described by Sir Nikolaus Pevsner as 'the stateliest house in the Close' and later occupied by the first physician at the infirmary. At the eastern end of the North Walk, near St. Ann's Gate, is Malmesbury House, another Georgian town house, whose ornamental plaster-work in a first floor room is more worthy of Horace Walpole's essay in the Gothic, Strawberry Hill, than a sedate and comfortable house in a cathedral close. On the south wall is a painted sundial, dated 1749, which bears the words 'Life is but a walking shadow'.

Many of the original buildings in the Close were improved or modified whilst the restoration work went on. The refacing of the medieval houses with classical façades and the introduction of new materials and techniques gradually re-shaped its character, and the re-building captures the sense of solid respectability which was beginning to typify Close life. But not all its residents were doctors or clergymen and, for a short while, part of the Vicars' Hall was occupied by the novelist, Henry Fielding and his first wife, one of the three beautiful Craddock sisters, all of whom had been born in Salisbury. It was here that Fielding wrote part of *Tom Jones*. But the behaviour of his household, 'in which wild extravagance and gorgeous velvet suits alternated with rags and the company of bailiffs', was not welcomed by his neighbours and the Fieldings' tenure was brief.

66

In 1727 Salisbury acquired its first street lamps. They were given to the city by one of its Members of Parliament and first lit to celebrate the coronation of George II. Four were erected in the Market Place, one on the Canal, one on both Fisherton and Crane Bridges, and the remaining sixteen were scattered through the city. Ten years later a Director of Highways was appointed to supervise street repairs, and the corporation began moving the street channels into new brick-lined conduits to allow more space for the passage of carts and carriages. Additional constables, a lamplighter and night-watchmen were appointed and the corporation ordered the population to refrain from throwing their refuse into the streets.

Looking south down Minster Street, a late eighteenth century engraving. The city's first street lamps were acquired in 1727; ten years later the street channels were moved into the brick conduits shown in this engraving.

A coffee house in the Market Place in 1782, by Thomas Rowlandson (1756–1827).

Benjamin Birch, an eighteenth century Salisbury chimney-sweep.

These first attempts at municipal improvement made little difference to the lives of Salisbury's craftsmen and tradesmen. The light from the street lamps was no match for the darkness of the winter months and link boys, carrying torches or lanterns, waited at the city gates to guide travellers to their lodgings. Prostitution and drunkenness flourished, and pickpockets and footpads haunted the narrow alleyways that ran between the tenement blocks. Piggeries, dung-heaps and cowstalls still filled the empty space behind the chequers. In the city's 100 inns the apprentices, carters and butchers gathered to drink their ale and risk their wages on dice, cockfighting and cudgelling. The cookshops that surrounded the Market Place were crowded with weavers and clothiers supping on local fare; Wiltshire hams, Wilton mutton, fish from the Avon and Southampton, venison from Cranborne Chase or the New Forest, hare and partridge hawked or netted on Salisbury Plain. For Salisbury, despite the activities of the gentry inside the Close, was still a country town. On market days it filled with livestock and carts, with farmers' wives come to sell their produce and refill their larders, with long trains of pack-horses, a bell tinkling from the neck of the leader, laden with bales of raw wool or bolts of finished cloth.

These were the things that gave Salisbury its character, that made it not just a cathedral city, but a natural focus for the villages of South Wiltshire. You could buy imported luxuries like china, carpets and tea in its shops. Criminals were brought to it to be hung and the sick to be healed. It was still rough and unsophisticated, but it was a robust and independent city in which business and pleasure freely intermingled. Its personalities were men like Mark Street, a 101-year-old saddler, Francis Atkins, porter at the North Gate who died aged 104, and 'the wonderful and surprising' English dwarf, who was only thirty-two inches tall, but who was 'shown to the Royal Family and most of the Nobility and Gentry of Great Britain.'

68

The cloth trade still dominated commercial life in the city. It employed perhaps a quarter of the population and Daniel Defoe, riding through Wiltshire in the 1710s, was amazed at the vast flocks of sheep that grazed the downland within twenty miles of the city. The wool was spun by women and children in the outlying villages and then brought to Salisbury to be dyed, woven, stretched and dried. Much of the output was broadcloth, but a few of the city weavers had begun specializing in a dark mottled marble-cloth used in dressmaking. A late eighteenth century trade directory lists twelve Salisbury clothiers and refers to the manufacture of flannels and fancy cloths for waistcoats, as well as serges, blanketings, cotton and a coarse linen called linsey, woven from a mixture of wool and flax.

The cloth trade suffered a series of depressions in the early part of the century which encouraged the development of other crafts. Of these lace-making, cutlery and leather-work were the most important. Aubrey mentions that Salisbury was 'ever famous' for its razors, knives and scissors, the quality of the steel being attributed to the chalk content in the local water. Nell Gwyn is reputed to have paid 100 guineas for a pair of Salisbury scissors and in 1784 a city cutler was appointed 'cutler to their Majesties'. Basketry, saddlery, parchment-making, shoemaking and malting also went on in the city, and Aubrey was convinced that it was the home of the 'best bottled ale in this nation'.

The city craftsmen easily outnumbered the rest of the population, but the increase in the number of gentry settling in the city had a gradual influence on its attitudes and way of life. They brought with them an appetite for comfort and the social graces of a provincial season, a taste for culture and refinement, which in time infected the middle-class clothiers who for so long had stood at the summit of Salisbury society. By the middle of the cen-

'The Wonderful and Surprising English Dwarf', born in Salisbury in 1709 and only thirty-two inches tall.

The eighteenth century trade card of William Wheeler, a Salisbury hatter and hosier.

An example of cutlery made in Salisbury and now preserved in Salisbury Museum.

James Harris (1709–1780); M.P. for Christchurch (1761–1765), during which period he held the offices of lord of the Admiralty and lord of the Treasury. Harris is now chiefly remembered for *Hermes, or a Philisophical Inquiry concerning the Universal Grammar* (1751).

The Council House, built in the Market Place in 1795 at the expense of the Earl of Radnor and now known as the Guildhall.

tury several coffee houses (of which the most fashionable was the Parade in Blue Boar Row), a theatre and two Assembly Rooms had opened their doors. By 1800 there was a literary society, a lending library, an archery society, and a social club for cards and conversation. After the final meeting at Salisbury Races a ball was held in the city, and fortnightly subscription concerts were given throughout the winter in the new Assembly Rooms on the corner of New Canal and the High Street.

The impetus for the gradual introduction of eighteenth century elegance into the city came from James Harris, owner of Malmesbury House from 1733 and father of the first Lord Malmesbury. His son thought he did much to 'improve and refine the taste and manners of the place', but Dr. Johnson described him as a 'prig and a bad prig'. Whatever the defects in Harris's character his wealth and position made him the natural leader of Salisbury society. He founded the annual music festival, held on St. Cecilia's Day in the cathedral and Assembly Rooms, and Handel is supposed to have played at one of his private concerts, given in a room above St. Ann's Gate.

Perhaps the most impressive result of the influx of the gentry was the construction of Salisbury Infirmary in Fisherton Street. In 1766, after Lord Radnor gave £500 for the purpose, a society was formed to promote the 'Relief of the Sick and Lame and Poor' in Wiltshire. Additional money was raised through subscription and two years later the new infirmary admitted its first patients. The medical staff consisted of two nurses, three visiting doctors and a matron and the daily diet was limited to bread, broth and three pints of beer. The infirmary was the first in Wiltshire and, although the original statutes stated that 'no woman big with child be admitted', it was proof of Salisbury's regional importance.

Another existing building belonging to the period is the Guildhall in the Market Place. In 1780 the Elizabethan Council House was destroyed by fire after the mayor's inaugural banquet. The city Recorder, the Earl of Radnor, offered to replace it at his own expense on condition that it was rebuilt in the middle of the Market Place to his design. This the corporation refused to allow and, after some dispute with the bishop, the Bishop's Guildhall was demolished and the present Guildhall erected on the site.

Salisbury's earliest newspaper, *The Salisbury Postman*, was first published in 1715. For 1½d. its readers received a summary of the week's 'intelligence, both Foreign and Domestick', and the sheets were pasted up on boards in the local towns and villages to encourage advertising. The *Postman* had a short life, but in 1729 a city printer, William Collins, brought out *The Salisbury Journal*. The paper, which is still published, was one of the first provincial newspapers in the country and its contents provide an evocative record of life in eighteenth century Salisbury.

The earliest issues of the paper contained articles on smallpox, poverty, the state of the streets, the wool tax and the need to widen the river to prevent flooding; all of them matters which had preoccupied the city since its medieval foundation: But by the late 1750s the eight page newspaper had found its own voice. It was highly critical of the Government (both Whig and Tory), unashamedly partisan in its reporting of local affairs, and happiest when discussing the activities of the local gentry. But perhaps its most striking feature was the amount of space devoted to crime. Felony and murder were both reported in muscular, unemotional eighteenth century prose, often with an editorial comment that the guilty, once apprehended, would reap their just reward. Many of these cases were national, the hanging of a highwayman at Tyburn or the 600 lashes given to each of three sailors for desertion, but the dispensation of local justice by the Wiltshire aristocracy in their capacity as Justices of the Peace makes gruesome, and often moving, reading. At the Summer Assize in 1758 seven prisoners were sent for trial from Fisherton Gaol. One was acquitted and four more were transported to Australia for fourteen years for theft. The death sentences passed on the other two prisoners reflect the inhumanity and hardship of the age. One was found guilty of horse stealing and the other, a young girl whose crime was more emotive than premeditated (she killed her illegitimate baby immediately after its birth), was eventually hung and her corpse exhibited in the Market Place.

Yet there was much in *The Salisbury Journal* of the late 1750s that evokes the vigour and exuberance of eighteenth century life. The paper's New Canal printing office sold books on domestic management, courtship and genteel behaviour, and, on the premise that 'it is impossible for the mind, however capacious, to remember all the Divisions of the several States and Kingdoms of the world', a 2/- map of the world; whilst for lighter reading it advertised such books as *The Fortunate Country Maid,* 'wherein are displayed the various and vile artifices employed by Men of Intrigue for seducing Young Women'. Its columns advertised patent medicines, contraband spirits seized from smugglers, carts, farms and horses 'free of all blemishes'. Its readers could claim the reward being offered by a 'gentleman of Sarum' whose purse had been snatched by footpads in Castle Street, or find employment as a 'man servant that has had smallpox, that understands shaving and dressing a wig, and looking after a couple of saddle horses'. Foreign and national news was inevitably slightly dated, but the 'latest intelligence' of the war with France – the Seven Years War had started in 1756 – was, whenever it was going well, assured a prominent headline on an inner page. The capture of Louisbourg by Wolfe in 1758 gave the corporation an excuse for celebration. Bells were rung, flags hoisted, a squadron of Dragoons fired a volley of muskets in the Market Place, and 'strong beer was given to rejoice the hearts of the Common People'. But the *Journal* was essentially a local paper and its pages reflected local interests: the enthronement of a new bishop, the price of corn and wool, the winter programme at the Assembly Rooms. A strain of parochial eccentricity ran through many of the stories it reported. The accidental death of an apprentice who fell from his horse whilst 'in liquor' and the dispute between a saddler and High Street shoe-

A drawing by Thomas Rowlandson, dated 1782, and entitled 'The Contest for Precedence over the Downs between Stockbridge and Salisbury.'

A rare caricature portrait of Gilbert Burnet, Bishop of Salisbury (1689–1715) and author of *Bishop Burnet's History of his own Time*. The words 'Lincey Woolsey', though derived from a form of inferior cloth, are here used to mean 'nonsensical', 'self-contradictory', 'neither one thing nor the other'.

A true blew Priest a Lincey Woolsey Brother –
One Legg a Pulpitt holds a Tubb the other
An Orthodox grave moderate Presbyterian –
Half Surplice Cloake half Priest half Puritan.
Made up of all these halfes hee cannot Pass.
For any thing intirely. but an Ass

maker over the ownership of a plum pudding were typical examples of city news. Tales of drunkenness were common. Perhaps the most remarkable in 1759 concerned a fire, caused by the negligence of a drunken carter, which destroyed a wagon laden with the 'Wardrobe, Scenery and Apparatus of the Bath Theatre, besides the entire Property and Wearing Apparel of each performer'.

From the outset the paper devoted a weekly column to the departure times of coaches to London and the West Country. As roads improved Salisbury consolidated its position as an important route centre and by 1773 52 coaches passed through the city each week. Competition between rival companies was fierce. Breakdowns and overturns were frequent and the presence of a red-coated guard armed with a blunderbuss, did not always deter highwaymen from holding up the coach as it crossed the downland that surrounds the city. Amongst the many coaches based on Salisbury were Robert Pouter's 'Flying Stage-Coach' which, for £1 and with five halts, reached London in twenty hours, and the 'Old Original Flying Machine hung on steel springs' which ran from Ludgate Hill to the Red Lion in Milford Street, performed, if God permits, by Anthony and John Croke'. By 1800 the number of daily coaches into Salisbury had increased to ten, amongst them a 'flyer coach' which covered the 84 miles between Salisbury and London in the then remarkable time of nine hours. Perhaps the most famous of the Salisbury coaches was the 'Quicksilver.' In 1783 it was held up by a highwayman, described by *The Salisbury Journal* as a 'savage robber' and characteristically dressed in a heavy greatcoat and oilskin hat; and in 1816 the guard was mauled by a lioness that had escaped from a private menagerie.

Salisbury's importance as a coaching centre led to the modernization of many of its inns. The White Hart in St. John's Street, rebuilt in 1790 with cream bricks made in Fisherton and designed like a country house, was probably the most fashionable posting-inn in the city. It was here that the gentry stayed when visiting the cathedral or returning to London from Weymouth, Exeter and the West Country. The increased use of heavier waggons and

72

larger coaches meant that many of the approach roads into the city had to be widened. Castle Street Gate was pulled down and Winchester Street Gate demolished to 'render entrance into the city spacious and convenient'. A reduction in turnpike tolls encouraged visitors and the toll on oxen hauling goods into the city was withdrawn.

The increase in road transport round Salisbury took place at the same time as a national improvement in the system of inland waterways. The barges plying the Avon had always been susceptible to sudden changes in the water level and in 1793 a scheme was put forward to link Salisbury to Southampton by canal. Work started immediately but, after absorbing £56,000, the canal had only reached West Dean on the Hampshire border. Attempts to raise extra capital failed and the canal was never completed.

For the most part Salisbury's eighteenth century bishops were mediocre prelates who owed their promotion to aristocratic connections or political patronage. Seth Ward's successor, Gilbert Burnet (1689-1715), re-awoke the traditional enmity between the bishop and corporation by interfering in city politics and befriending Nonconformists. Benjamin Hoadly (1723-1734) was one of the most controversial churchmen of his day. His supporters thought him a champion of the 'natural, civil and religious rights of all Englishmen' and his critics a 'singularly unpleasant example of a pompous, worldly, latitudinarian divine of the eighteenth century'. The theological storms that raged round Hoadly throughout his career are outside the scope of this book, but his engraving by Hogarth depicts a Pickwickian looking cleric comfortably seated on his bishop's throne. The most uncontroversial of Salisbury's eighteenth century bishops was undoubtedly John Thomas (1761-1766). Bishop Thomas's marital affairs dissipated much of his energy. He outlived his first three wives and attributed the shortness of their lives to the fact that he always allowed them their own way. Inscribed on his fourth wedding ring was the motto 'If I survive, I'll make them five': a few months later he was dead.

'The Departure from the "White Hart", Salisbury, attended by Landlord, Waiters, Chambermaids, Postboys, Hostlers, etc. etc., who never fail attending the departure of Guests, however badly attended to during their stay at the Inn'; by Thomas Rowlandson.

ABOVE RIGHT A post-chaise notice.

Benjamin Hoadly, Bishop of Salisbury (1723–1734), an engraving from the portrait by William Hogarth. The two men were great friends, and Hoadly's letters to Hogarth reveal a wit and humour of which few of his contemporaries were aware.

Salisbury Cathedral in 1754. Looking east down the nave towards the thirteenth century choir screen demolished by James Wyatt circa 1789.

In 1782 Shute Barrington was enthroned Bishop of Salisbury and seven years later he invited the architect James Wyatt to advise him on the restoration of the cathedral and the Close. Wyatt was one of the leading architects of his day. He designed the cloisters at Wilton House for the Earl of Pembroke and Fonthill Abbey for William Beckford, and much has been written, most of it uncomplimentary, about his work in Salisbury. He has been described as 'destructive', as the 'perpetrator of a hideous and prolonged practical joke', and accused of 'wanton injury' and 'capricious innovation'. In his efforts to preserve the architectural unity of the cathedral's interior Wyatt re-arranged or removed anything that was inconsistent with his vision of the authentic Gothic cathedral. He was determined to simplify its internal design and began his work by moving the tombs into neat lines between the columns in the nave. He whitewashed the vaulted ceiling to hide the now faded medieval colouring and then, to let more light into the cathedral, removed the remaining thirteenth century stained glass, replacing it with clear glazing (the original glass was broken up and dumped in the Close ditch). Wyatt's most criticized 'improvement' was the destruction of two fifteenth century chantry chapels, in memory of Bishop Beauchamp and Robert, Lord Hungerford, which had been built into the walls on either side of the Trinity Chapel at the cathedral's eastern end. The Beauchamp Chantry had a carved oak ceiling and the bishop and both his parents lay in marble canopied tombs. The Hungerford Chantry had suffered badly from damp and neglect, but its walls were covered in medieval paintings. Wyatt's intention was to restore the cathedral's outline to its original design, but the superb painted fan tracery in the surviving Audley Chantry emphasizes the tragedy of their destruction. The architect's other major internal restoration work was equally capricious. He removed the choir fittings designed by

The interior of the Hungerford Chapel, founded in 1464 by Margaret, the widow of Robert, Lord Hungerford, on the north side of the Trinity Chapel. The chantry, and its superb wall paintings, was destroyed by Wyatt in 1789; the alabaster effigy of Lord Hungerford now lies in the nave.

74

The richly decorated interior of the Beauchamp Chapel, the chantry chapel founded by Richard Beauchamp, Bishop of Salisbury (died 1481), on the south side of the Trinity Chapel. After Wyatt demolished the chapel the bishop's tomb was 'mislaid' and his remains were placed in an unmarked tomb, which Wyatt transplanted from the north transept to the nave.

Wren and demolished the delicate thirteenth century stone screen which divided the choir from the nave. A new screen was built, partly out of the remnants of the Beauchamp and Hungerford Chantries, and an organ given to the cathedral by George III was placed on top.

Wyatt's work in the Close was more successful. The small ditches that crossed it were 'foul and stinking' and the cathedral was liable to flooding. In 1782 the Close was described by a visitor as being 'as dirty and neglected as a cow-common, and through the centre stagnates a boggy ditch'. Wyatt drained, levelled and raised the entire Close. Prior to his arrival much of it had been meadow grazed by cattle, and the open expanse of lawn that now surrounds the cathedral is perhaps his finest legacy. Sadly, when raising the level of the Close, Wyatt covered up the tombs and graves in the churchyard. The corporation protested and refused financial assistance for the work, but Bishop Barrington sided with his architect and only a plan, preserved in the Muniment Room, remains to mark the position of the graves. Wyatt's final act in the Close was the demolition of the medieval belfry that then stood to the north of the cathedral. It was not entirely his fault. As early as 1757 the chapter had decided that neither its tower or spire were 'useful or ornamental', and in 1768 the 200 foot spire was pulled down. Part of the belfry had been in regular use as a tavern since before the Reformation and two of the bells were badly cracked. In 1790 Wyatt ordered the belfry to be demolished and all but the sixth bell to be sold. The clock mechanism and remaining bell were installed in the central tower of the cathedral and, in 1884, the clock was moved to the north aisle. The bell is still in use, whilst the clock is thought to be the oldest in working order in England.

Wyatt's work was finished in 1792 and that year George III, his queen and five princesses visited the cathedral to inspect the results. According to the account of their visit in *The Salisbury Journal* 'their Majesties inspected the improvements with minute attention and much satisfaction, not only at the

The cathedral and belfry, from an
engraving dated 1761.

elegance and propriety of each, but also at the boldly striking, yet simple and
singularly beautiful effect of the tout ensemble'. The opinion of the royal
family has not been shared by most subsequent visitors to the cathedral, and
both Wyatt and Bishop Barrington must share responsibility for the criticism
of their work. It is hard to be objective about the success or failure of their
attempt to recapture the cathedral's medieval character. But the destruction
of the two chantries, the stained glass, the choir screen, the belfry and the re-
arranging of the tombs, robbed Salisbury Cathedral of much that was vital
to its spiritual, historical and physical unity. Perhaps the best that can be said
is that their improvements re-emphasized the clarity and simplicity of the
cathedral's original design.

By the end of the eighteenth century Salisbury had mellowed into a quiet
cathedral city enjoyed by the gentry and essential to the way of life of South
Wiltshire. In 1796 England declared war on France. The start of the Napoleonic Wars led to a depression in the cloth trade from which the city never
recovered. The corporation must have sensed that the war might mark the
end of an era. For in a petition to the king, pleading for peace, they described
it as being 'carried on by an unexampled profusion of public money, and a
system of delusion and corrupt influence, which threatens the subversion of
the principles of our conduct'. By 1815, when victory at Waterloo was celebrated with a public dinner in the Market Place, Salisbury's commercial importance was minimal and its future bleak.

76

SIX

A Fair Old City

And that soaring spire which, rising so high above the red town, first catches the eye, the one object which gives unity and distinction to the whole picture, is not more distinct in the mind than the entire Salisbury with its manifold interests and activities.

W. H. HUDSON *A Shepherd's Life*, 1910

In the early pages of *Martin Chuzzlewit* Charles Dickens described mid-Victorian Salisbury.

Mr. Pinch had a shrewd notion that Salisbury was a very desperate sort of place; an exceedingly wild and dissipated city; and when he had put up the horse, and given the hostler to understand that he would look in again in the course of an hour or two to see him take his corn, he set forth on a stroll about the streets with a vague and not unpleasant idea that they teemed with all kinds of mystery and bedevilment. To one of his quiet habits this little delusion was greatly assisted by the circumstance of its being market-day, and the thorough-fares about the market-place being filled with carts, horses, donkeys, baskets, waggons, garden-stuff, meat, tripe, pies, poultry, and hucksters' wares of every opposite description and possible variety of character. Then there were young farmers and old farmers, with smock-frocks, brown great-coats, drab great-coats, red worsted comforters, leather leggings, wonderful shaped hats, hunting whips, and rough sticks, standing about in groups, or talking noisily together on the tavern steps, or paying and receiving huge amounts of greasy wealth, with the assistance of such bulky pocket-books that when they were in their pockets it was apoplexy to get them out, and when they were out, it was spasms to get them in again. Also there were farmers' wives in beaver bonnets and red cloaks, riding shaggy ponies purged of all earthly passions, who went soberly into all manner of places without desiring to know why, and who, if required, would have stood stock still in a china shop, with a complete dinner-service at each hoof. Also a great many dogs, who were strongly interested in the state of the market and the bargains of their masters; and a great confusion of tongues, both brute and human.

After buying a pocket-knife from a cutler Tom Pinch continued on his tour of the city, passing its theatre and only bank and gazing through the windows of the High Street shops. In the late afternoon he went into the cathedral and up into the organ-loft. He was a friend of the assistant organist and, after evening service had been celebrated, he sat at the organ and filled the empty building with its 'grand tones'. After leaving the cathedral Tom returned through the lamp-lit streets to the tavern where he had stabled his horse. Then, pulling his table close to the parlour fire, he 'fell to work upon a well-cooked steak and smoking hot potatoes' washed down with a jug of 'most stupendous Wiltshire beer'.

In this long and evocative passage Dickens captured the essence of Victorian Salisbury. For the Market Place, cathedral, shops and inns guaranteed the city's survival in the years that followed the decline and disappearance of the cloth trade. The nineteenth century was to be one of paradox. For despite the lack of major industry in an age which gave first priority to industrial growth, Salisbury's population rose steadily. Between 1800 and 1900 it climbed from under 8,000 to nearly 16,000. By 1953 it had reached 32,000 and the housing estates and Victorian villas which now surround three sides of the medieval city are a permanent reminder of the city's expansion.

Yet throughout the first half of the nineteenth century life in South Wiltshire was characterized by widespread unrest and poverty. The spread of the Speenhamland system, of paying poor relief to supplement wages, demoralized and pauperized the rural labourer. The decline of cottage industries, the introduction of harsher game laws, and the continued enclosure of the common land, gradually robbed the agricultural worker of his independence, status and livelihood. William Cobbett's description of his rural ride down the Avon valley contains a savage indictment of the decay and poverty that had befallen the area. 'In taking my leave of this beautiful vale, I have to express my deep shame as an Englishman at beholding the general extreme poverty of those who caused this vale to produce such quantities of food and raiment. This is, I verily believe it, the worst used labouring people upon the face of the earth. Dogs and hogs and horses are treated with more civility'.

The lack of interest in the plight of the labourer resulted in occasional outbreaks of violence, much of it directed against the new agricultural and manufacturing machinery that had made them redundant. In 1830 the farm workers of South Wiltshire rioted. After wrecking a threshing machine at Bishopsdown Farm they marched on Salisbury to destroy Figes's Iron Foundry. The Riot Act was read out in the Green Croft and the rioters were dispersed by the Wiltshire Yeomanry. At a special assize held afterwards 322 prisoners were sent for trial. Twenty-eight were transported for life; a figure which indicates the seriousness with which the local gentry regarded the situation.

The decline of the cloth trade and the unrest in the countryside had its repercussions inside Salisbury. The granting of poor relief and attempts to aid the unemployed through municipal improvement schemes made little impression on their number. The Crane Street workhouse was permanently full. It fed and clothed over 200 paupers whose daily diet consisted of 1 lb of bread, $1\frac{1}{2}$ ozs. of cheese and $1\frac{3}{4}$ ozs. of meat each. It was constantly criticized for mismanagement and the report of the Poor Law Commission in 1834 emphasized its shortcomings. The building was dilapidated, the elderly master was confined to his chair by gout and rheumatism, and the commissioners

stated that they had never seen 'a more disgusting scene of filth and mis-rule than the Salisbury workhouse'. The problems faced by the corporation were exaggerated by the large numbers of beggars who continued to roam the streets. In 1818 a group of local worthies, who believed, with some jus-tification, that the city beggars spread disease and diverted funds from more deserving charities, founded the Salisbury Society for the Suppression of Mendicity. Two lodging houses were established and, instead of alms, beg-gars were given tickets which provided them with food and shelter for one night. By 1840 the lodging houses were admitting over 5,000 paupers a year.

The widespread unemployment inside the city and the discontent outside it led to an inevitable increase in the local crime rate. At a time when even the theft of a twopenny loaf of bread carried a sentence of life-imprisonment the county goal in Fisherton Street was obviously inadequate, and early in the nineteenth century a new prison was built at the junction of the Devizes and Wilton roads. It contained a bridewell, a debtors' ward and seven yards for differing classes of prisoner. It was from the gallows outside the new prison that a Robert Watkins was publicly hung in 1819 for the murder of a city coal-merchant before a crowd of 15,000. In its account of the hanging *The Salisbury & Winchester Journal* reported that the performance of the hang-man's 'grim office' was followed by a thunderstorm, 'which struck terror in

Salisbury from Old Sarum, from a drawing by J. M. W. Turner (1775–1851).

Salisbury Cathedral by John
Constable, painted from inside
the grounds of the Bishop's
Palace.

a good many, and greatly impressed everybody present on this solemn occasion of the satisfying of justice'. The last public hanging in Salisbury took
place in 1855, but by then only a few people were willing to watch as the
'wretched man was launched into eternity'. The growing humanitarianism
of the age had made it less tolerant of public spectacle and three years later
the stocks in the Market Place were employed for the final time. After being
found guilty of drunkenness, for the eighth time in fourteen months, a John
Selloway was placed in them for six hours.

Despite the many problems which faced Salisbury in the early years of the
nineteenth century it remained a peaceful and respectable city in which shopkeepers, clergymen and the gentry could go about their business. The corres-
pondence between the painter John Constable and John Fisher, Archdeacon
of Berkshire, carried on between 1812 and 1830, describes a pleasant and
somnolent way of life on which poverty and hardship rarely impose. Fisher,
whose uncle was Bishop of Salisbury, was one of Constable's earliest friends
and patrons, and his letters to the painter are full of anecdotes about the
somewhat small preoccupations and emotions which were beginning to characterize Close life. He described his fellow clergy as typified by a 'full blown
wig, deep shovel hat, apron, round belly, double chin, stern eye, rough
voice, and imperious manner, drinking port wine and laying down the law

of the best way for escaping the Curates Residence Act'. In another letter to Constable he remarked on the ecclesiastical fondness for a well-spread table: 'So belly devoted are the good people here, that they look upon it as a sort of *duty* imposed on the canons in residence, to dine out or give a dinner every day as punctually as one goes to church'.

But Fisher himself had no time for the more trivial idiosyncrasies of Close life. He too was something of an artist and, when Constable came to stay, the two men would stride out into the country laden with drawing-books, inks, paintboxes and brushes. Constable's paintings of Stonehenge, Harnham Bridge and Old Sarum all date from his first visit to Salisbury in 1812, and from then on he was a frequent guest at the Leadenhall, the Fishers' home in the Close. In *Salisbury Cathedral from the Water Meadows*, painted in 1830 and turned into a masterpiece by the addition of a rainbow, he captured a beauty and tranquillity that still survives, particularly if one looks back at the Close from the west bank of the Avon. This world of water and meadows was one that Constable loved. In a letter to Fisher he once wrote: 'But the sound of water escaping over from mill dams, willows and rotten planks, slimy posts and brickworks – I love such things'.

By the middle of the nineteenth century Salisbury had acquired most of the benefits (and some of the defects) offered by the Industrial Revolution to the larger provincial cities. Gas lighting was introduced in 1833. The more nervous thought it likely to lead to suffocation, poisoning, explosion or fire, and 'many were the forebodings of the evil that would result from its use'. The arrival of Brunel's Great Western Railway in 1856, linking Salisbury with Warminster and Bristol, had much greater significance for the city's future and, on this occasion, the worst fears of the timid were soon to be realized. Salisbury's first rail link had been established in 1847 when the Salisbury & Bishopstoke Railway opened its Milford Station to goods traffic. Within a few months it began carrying passengers. A 1st class return ticket to London cost 24/- and the service took four hours to reach the capital, thus halving the time taken by the fastest coach. Cheap excursion tickets were soon available and by the mid-1850s Salisbury's coaching days were over. The effect of the railways on the city was permanent. Apart from opening up communications and making the city less parochial it gave fresh impetus to trade and encouraged an increasing number of middle class settlers to move in. The small village of Fisherton Anger was the first casualty. Many of the new residents built trim suburban villas in the streets round Fisherton Station; the well-to-do acquired mock-Gothic mansions on the northern edge of the city, an area that had a reputation for having a 'healthy character'. The outward march of the suburbs had begun: between 1835 and 1954 the city extended its boundaries five times.

Brunel's roofed-over station at Fisherton closed to passenger traffic in 1932. Sadly, it is now going derelict, but it was here, four months after the line opened in 1856, that Salisbury discovered that the steam engine was as prone to disaster as the slowest of its predecessors. A cattle train, pulled by two engines, ploughed through the buffers and wooden platform and demolished the ladies' waiting room. The leading engine came to a halt when parallel with the street and the fortunate driver escaped unharmed. But the second engine and the cattle waggons behind it piled one into the other and 'all was dismay, confusion, perplexity and darkness'. 'It is almost impossible', wrote the reporter from *The Salisbury & Winchester Journal*, 'to describe the scene which ensued: the gas was extinguished, fearing that some accident might accrue therefrom, and the only lights available were a few candles and dark lanterns: and the crowds of people which had assembled on the platform were tumbling over each other. The foremost engine emitted large volumes of steam, which filled the station and rendered the light less visible. Flames of fire were then discovered, which were caused by the timber of the floorings becoming ignited by the fire from the engine'. Add to this the tearful shrieks of the occupants of the ladies' waiting room, the lowing of cattle and bleating of sheep and the scene can perhaps be imagined. Remarkably, the fire was soon under control and, although most of the livestock on board the train perished, there were only two human casualties.

A year later the London & South Western Railway opened a direct line to London and a new station was built at Fisherton alongside Brunel's terminus. It was to be the site of the worst railway accident in Salisbury's history. In 1906 a boat train, travelling to London from Plymouth, entered the station at speed, collided with a stationary goods train, left the rails and plunged over Fisherton Bridge. Twenty-eight people died – many of them Americans and Canadians, a plaque to their memory being erected in the cathedral – and, for many years afterwards, Salisbury was a compulsory halt for all trains passing through the city.

Salisbury had a third, internal railway. In 1859 a Mr. Strapp designed a Market House which was built at the western end of the Market Place. Its vast open space, wrought iron galleries, glass roof and three stone arches divided by 'rusticated Tuscan piers' were reminiscent of Crystal Palace. The Market House was connected to Fisherton Station by a full-gauge railway and the new building symbolized the city's mid-Victorian prosperity. It was

The scene at Fisherton Station after the 1906 railway disaster.

soon renamed the Corn Exchange and in *A Shepherd's Life* W. H. Hudson described it as a 'huge beehive, humming with the noise of talk, full of brown-faced farmers in their riding and driving clothes and leggings, standing in knots or thrusting their hands into sacks of oats and barley'. It was never a great commercial success. The railway closed in 1918, the stallholders returned to their traditional pitches in the Market Place and by 1950 it stood empty and neglected, a dilapidated venue for cat-shows and wrestling. In 1975 it reopened as Salisbury Divisional Library, but the elegant façade was preserved.

The mid-nineteenth century was a period of expansion and reform. The boundaries of the medieval city blurred and many of its links with the past were severed. The disappearance of the thirteenth century street channels was typical of the changes that took place within the city. During the 1820s and 1830s many were arched over; for 'neither art nor nature', wrote the city medical officer, 'could have formed channels better adapted for effectually carrying away the sewage of the city'. He was soon proved wrong. In 1849 a cholera epidemic killed 234 people in six months. The street channels were blamed and immediately uncovered. But the city's sanitary arrangements were far from satisfactory. The sub-soil in the gardens behind the chequers was saturated with filth, many of the wells were contaminated, and the continued presence of cess-pits, piggeries, dung-heaps and an open sewage system increased the risk of a second outbreak of cholera. During the 1850s a new sewage system was dug (until 1881 the sewage was untreated and pumped directly into the Avon) and the Close ditch and street

Mr. Strapp's Salisbury Market House, now the Central Library, from *The Illustrated London News* (June 1859). The railway entered the Market House on the left.

83

A Salisbury trade exhibition in the Banqueting Room of the Guildhall in 1852, the year after the Great Exhibition had opened in the Crystal Palace in London.

channels were filled in. When the Canal was filled in in 1875 the city's 600-year-old reputation for being an English Venice was finally laid to rest.

One result of the destruction of the street channels was the establishment of Salisbury's first museum in St. Ann Street to house the relics that had been found in them. In 1867 William Blackmore opened a second museum in St. Ann Street to display his private collection of early Mexican and American antiquities. In 1904 the two museums merged, and today Salisbury Museum is widely regarded as one of the most important provincial museums in the country.

The arrival of the railways and the disappearance of the street channels were an undoubted benefit to nineteenth century Salisbury. The defects of progress are less tangible and harder to define, but they none the less existed. Apart from the proliferation of innumerable identical red brick houses on the rim of the city, they belong to the realm of social attitudes and behaviour. A hint of the change can be found in Robert Benson's and Henry Hatcher's *History of Salisbury*, first published in 1843. In describing eighteenth century working class behaviour they wrote: 'the lower orders were then more respectful to their superiors, more decorous in their manner, more faithful to their services, than they are unfortunately found to be at present'. They were wrong, but they chose to pretend otherwise. For the truth is that Salisbury, like every other provincial city in England, was beginning to mirror the rigid ethos of the age. The pursuit of wealth to the exclusion of almost every other worldly pleasure sapped its individuality and vivacity. It grew sober, industrious and self-righteous; a city of solemn successful merchants, Victorian matrons in voluminous skirts who only relaxed when croqueting 'the curate pitilessly into the geraniums', clergymen in perpendicular black hats and gentry with private means. The *History of Salisbury* mentions that the 'habit of tippling' had become a thing of the past. How could it otherwise when that most enduring memorial to medieval Salisbury, the Old George Inn, had been turned into a Temperance Hotel? It was a city in which men like John Hall would have been ill-at-ease, for the social hierarchy had no place for a man whose fortune had been founded on trade. The private schools in the Close, dedicated to the production of 'Young Ladies' who would be 'lovely to Society and pleasing to themselves', placed emphasis in their advertisements on such key Victorian nouns as Virtue and Sentiment, Morality and Maturity. The genuine piety of the middle-class family was exaggerated by the presence of the cathedral and the large number of clergymen who lived in the city. Bibles were chained to reading desks in the station waiting rooms for the waiting traveller to consult. The cathedral chapter employed a woman whose sole duty was to remove the daisies from the Close lawns; its dust was laid by water carts which toured its walks before the residents awoke. It was a world that is now extinct, and one must turn to Hardy's *Jude the Obscure* and the novels of Trollope for an understanding of the morality and behaviour of nineteenth century Salisbury.

And yet the city had not completely forgotten how to enjoy itself. The proximity of the countryside and the continual coming and going of farmers, carters and farm labourers guaranteed the survival of many of its traditional habits. At Christmas Jenny-Jacks begged and danced in the streets. Fairs were held in the Close in April and October. Then the outlying villagers flocked into the city to spend their harvest money, and many of the shopkeepers provided free luncheons for their customers. There were gypsy caravans, wild beast shows, boxing matches and avenues of stalls which sold everything from Staffordshire fairings to the latest turnip cutter. On public holidays the population embarked in carriers' carts and picnicked on eels,

85

whitebait, haunches of mutton, tarts and custard at Stonehenge, the Larmer Tree Grounds and on Harnham Hill. But the public dinners held in the Market Place whenever the excuse for celebration presented itself were perhaps the best proof that the city's spirit was still intact. After the fall of Sevastopol 7,000 men sat down at trestle tables to a meal of beef and beer. During Queen Victoria's Jubilee Celebrations in 1887 the 'grand old Market Place' again echoed to 'the sound of cutlery, the chinking of glasses, and the merry chatter of the diners', and the mayor's father proudly announced that he could remember attending a similar dinner for George III's Jubilee in 1809. At Edward VII's Coronation Dinner in 1902 250 carvers were needed to feed the 4,000 who attended. By the time the meal was over 2 tons of beef, 1,600 lb of pudding and 800 gallons of beer had been consumed. In the afternoon 4,000 women 'did justice' to a ton of cake and 50 lb of tea.

In about 1870 Sir Gilbert Scott was invited to re-design the interior of the cathedral, with the result that most of Wyatt's improvements were removed. George III's organ was given to St. Thomas's Church, the choir screen was replaced by an open metal screen, the choir stalls were taken out and a new Gothic floor was laid. When working in the cathedral Scott also destroyed a series of life size charcoal drawings of soldiers on the cloister walls, drawn by a member of the Wiltshire Volunteers when they were being used as a drill ground during the Napoleonic Wars.

Gilbert Scott's improvements have proved too fussy for contemporary tastes. His screen has since been removed – leaving an uninterrupted view down the length of the cathedral, and the Trinity Chapel and choir have been re-paved and re-furnished. The cathedral is now probably in better condition than at any other time in its history. In 1950 £20,000 was spent on re-placing the capstone and uppermost thirty feet of the spire and adding

The public dinner in the Market Place to celebrate the Coronation of Edward VII in 1902.

aircraft warning lights, and three new stained glass windows have recently been inserted on the north side of the nave.

The gradual restoration of the cathedral underlines its continued importance to Salisbury as a regional centre of worship. Ever since the episcopacy of Seth Ward its prestige has increased and it is now one of the most enduring symbols of the Anglican faith. But strangely enough, the nineteenth century, for all its narrow-mindedness and constraint, marked the arrival of various other Christian denominations in the city. Augustus Pugin, who himself lived close to the city and restored John Hall's house in New Canal, designed the Roman Catholic church of St. Osmund's in Exeter Street. By 1900 the Presbyterians, Methodists, Congregationalists, Catholic Apostolic Church, Open Christian Brethren, Christian Scientists, Swedenborgians, Christadelphians, New Jerusalemists and Elim Four-Square Gospel Alliance all had halls or chapels in the city. Salisbury's religious reputation would seem to have attracted some of the more eccentric forms of Christian worship. How else can one describe Mrs Girling and her 'Shakers' who in 1875 held a series of meetings in the city? She was accompanied by eight women and four men, all of them dressed in white. At one meeting one of the women started clapping and dancing, another shouted 'Carry me home with my burden' and the others began whimpering and groaning. 'The audience', wrote *The Salisbury & Winchester Journal*, 'was much struck with these manifestations.' Members of the Salvation Army began preaching in the city in 1881. Their 'aggressive and uncompromising attitude' won them few converts, the mayor forbade them to meet and a Society for the Suppression of Street Parades was organized in opposition. On one occasion a crowd of over 1,000 pelted them with eggs and tomatoes and used 'bludgeons and other formidable weapons, and attacked defenceless women as well as men'.

The various churches in late nineteenth century Salisbury were easily outnumbered by the skills and crafts that still flourished in the city. It was then considerably more self-sufficient than it is today and the trade directories from the period reflect the enterprise of its craftsmen and shopkeepers. In 1897 it boasted 25 bakers, 9 breweries, 8 coachbuilders, 10 dairies, 13 hatters, 22 shoemakers, 9 piano tuners, 3 millers, 25 pastrycooks, as well as saddlers, dyers, a cork cutter, bell hanger, cabinet maker, coopers, wheelwrights, smiths, sweeps, a soda water manufacturer, cutlers, drapers, a pawnbroker and such unlikely gentlemen as the proprietor of a Turkish Bath, a professor of dancing and deportment and the owner of a flea circus.

This diversity is echoed in the advertisements that appeared towards the end of the directories. Amongst the goods sold in the city shops were rabbit and sparrow nets, leggings, 'Hussey's Celebrated Malt Liquors', 'Outfits for the Colonies and Clerical Garments', 'Hunts Herbal Remedies', toilet requisites, patent medicines, 'Hart's Safety Cycling Skirt', cooking ranges and a non-alcoholic cider recommended for 'cricket matches, garden parties, clergymen and Temperance Banquets'. Its inns offered 'good beds and stabling', meals of 'astounding value' and 'well-ventilated laundry'.

A twenty-seven seater Scout charabanc.

A Scout van belonging to Robert Stokes, a Salisbury tea and coffee merchant.

Despite the profusion of goods and talent there was still widespread unemployment in the city, particularly round Fisherton Station – an area that had slowly lost its initial respectability. In harsh winters coal and groceries were distributed to the poor and free soup and fish kitchens were set up on street corners. There were many attempts to develop new industries and reduce unemployment. The Invicta Leather Works in Endless Street now stand empty, but they were often cited as an example of 'what can be accomplished by skill, energy and enterprise'. The Scout Motor Company was perhaps the only industry in the city that might have had a permanent effect on its character. The company was founded in 1902 to make motor-boat engines by a Salisbury clockmaker, Albert Burden. The production of cars soon followed and when Burden moved the works out to Bemerton in 1907 he was employing 70 men and making two cars a week. Only two Scout cars are now known to exist, but the company's early advertisements must have helped them find a ready market: 'How to Fly, purchase a Scout Car. They simply fly up hills in top gear and skim along the ground like a bird'. In 1912 one of them touched 52 miles an hour over a measured mile on Salisbury Plain. Each car was built to rally standards and the 6 cylinder 30 horse power model cost £285 and came complete with reverse gear, brass headlights and leather upholstery. The change to the production of mines during the First World War crippled the company's output. It was unable to compete with the cheaper mass-production cars beginning to come on to the market and production finally stopped in 1922.

Perhaps the most revolutionary vehicles made by the company were its charabancs. These served a dual purpose, for when the long inward facing seats that lined the side were folded up the empty space could be used for carrying milk churns or grain. They were operated by private carrier services and soon brought Salisbury into closer contact with the isolated villages on the Plain. As distances were reduced, the importance of Salisbury as a marketing and shopping centre increased. The Market Place had always been Salisbury's commercial heart, for it had survived the lean as well as the prosperous years and in the process acquired a social character that was peculiarly its own. W. H. Hudson's description of it in *A Shepherd's Life* cannot be improved.

Business is business and must attended to, in fair or foul weather, but for business with pleasure we prefer it fine on market-day. The one great and chief pleasure, in which we all participate, is just to be there, to be in the crowd – a joyful occasion which gives a festive look to every face. The mere sight of it exhilarates like wine. The numbers – the people and the animals! The carriers' carts drawn up in rows on rows – carriers from a hundred little villages on the Bourne, the Avon, the Wylye, the Nadder, the Ebble, and from all over the Plain, each bringing its little contingent. Hundreds and hundreds more coming by train; you see them pouring down Fisherton Street in a continuous procession, all hurrying marketwards. And what a lively scene the market presents now, full of cattle and sheep and pigs and crowds of people standing round the shouting auctioneers! And horses, too the beribboned hacks and ponderous draught horses with manes and

The Market Place in the late nineteenth century.

tails decorated with golden straw, thundering over the stone pavement as they are trotted up and down! And what a profusion of fruit and vegetables, fish and meat, and all kinds of provisions on the stalls, where women with baskets on their arms are jostling and bargaining!

When Hudson wrote those words in 1910 the Market Place still symbolized the agricultural way of life that had existed in South Wiltshire since time immemorial. But the twentieth century was to bring a new purpose to much of the downland that divides the two halves of the county. The military occupation of Salisbury Plain had first been suggested in 1872 when the first large-scale military manoeuvres were held in the area. They were staged with all the pomp and splendour that imperial Britain could muster. The cavalry charged, the red-coated infantry formed the frail squares that had won them victory under Wellington and, after the manoeuvres were over, the 20,000 soldiers who had taken part were reviewed by the Prince of Wales A crowd, estimated at 100,000, gathered on Beacon Hill to 'feast their eyes on a scene of stirring martial brilliance and magnificence'. Nearly thirty years were to elapse before the military occupation of the Plain became a reality. The outbreak of the Boer War made it essential for army exercises to take place over a terrain similar to the South African veldt, and in 1897 the government bought 750 acres near Bulford. Later that year £450,000 was spent on the purchase of a further 60 square miles of downland. The first barracks were built at Tidworth in 1902 and nine years later an Air Battalion attached to the Royal Artillery established a base at Larkhill.

The arrival of large numbers of troops in the area brought new prosperity to Salisbury and the city inns were soon crowded with soldiers. Long lines of canvas appeared on the downland and in the skies above the Plain aeroplanes could be seen 'soaring, swooping and wheeling in all directions, while the air was full of the droning, hum of their engines.'

With the outbreak of the First World War in 1914 Salisbury Plain became the largest military encampment in England, and the arrival of young soldiers from the furthest corners of the Empire soon blew away the last residues of Victorian decorum. The city women put down their tapestry work and began knitting the comforters, gloves and socks needed by the troops. The training battalions in 'Kitchener's Army' spent that first, bitterly cold winter of the war under canvas, neglected by the War Office and often without blankets or proper food. They were only 'too eager to motor into Salisbury over miles of ruined roads for a little change and fun and select female company': an activity that prompted its citizens to form a special Women's Patrol to protect the virtue of their womenfolk. For the next four years the muddy lanes round the city were to be clogged with traction engines, baggage trains and squads of soldiers in ill-fitting tunics who sang as they marched:

> 'Why did we join the Army, boys?
> Why did we join the Army?
> Why did we come to Salisbury Plain?
> We must have been ruddy well barmy!'

In 1939 the songs were different but the sentiments and scene much the same. Convoys rumbled through the blacked-out city streets, the Home Guard spent the winter nights on lookout duty and the women went to work in canteens, munition factories and on the land. Much of Salisbury Plain was handed over to the Americans and in the months before D-Day it became a training area and staging post.

In May 1945 peace returned to Europe. Salisbury's streets were decorated with flags, girls wore ribbon in their hair, church bells pealed, sirens sounded and 3,000 people attended a Thanksgiving Service in the cathedral. By late evening the streets were filled with revellers, for 'the gaiety had increased as the day wore on, staid citizens and others not so staid were ready to dance. Public houses remained open till midnight, when the merrymakers, arm in arm and still singing, made their way home'.

The impact of the twentieth century on Salisbury's character is still hard to gauge. The depression of the early Thirties brought the soup kitchen back into its streets, but an influx of light manufacturing and marketing industries in the post-war years has helped the city to maintain its prosperity. The population continues to rise. But although the city has absorbed the villages of Milford, Bemerton and Harnham the new housing develeopments have, on the whole, blended well with the character of the medieval city. The Ministry of Defence still occupy much of Salisbury Plain and the location of the headquarters of the United Kingdom Land Forces at Wilton has strengthened the city's military links. The Close and Market Place remain virtually unchanged, though the livestock market has been moved to a new site and extensions to the College of Sarum St. Michael have provided the Close with a hint of the twentieth century. The biggest threat to the character of the city centre has come from the inevitable increase in traffic. The medieval street pattern was not designed for the demands of the modern city, and the provision of car parks and a ring-road seem to have made little difference to the density of traffic in the streets round the Market Place.

But Salisbury's prestige continues to rise and conservation of its spiritual and architectural heritage has become even more important now that it has developed into a major regional tourist centre. The conversion of the Corn Exchange into the new Central Library, the building of a new Playhouse and the establishment of an annual Salisbury Festival have perhaps helped the city regain its vitality. But whatever the future might hold in store Salisbury's heart remains unmistakably the same. Its prosperity continues to depend on the cathedral and commerce, and visitors still enter the Close through the gates used by the medieval pilgrims. The spire still soars above the tile-hung houses that surround the Market Place, and through the streets flows a river that has been journeying to the sea since long before Richard Poore and one hundred settlers exchanged Old Sarum for a new city 'where the valleys abound in corn and the fields are beautiful'.

Bibliography

Aubrey, John *Brief Lives* ed. Powell (1949)
  The Natural History of Wiltshire (1969)
Beckett, R. B. (ed.) *John Constable and the Fishers* (1952)
Benson, Robert & Hatcher, Henry *Old and New Sarum or Salisbury* (1843)
Britton, John *The Beauties of England and Wales* Vol. XV, Wiltshire (1814)
Bryant, Arthur *The Story of England, Makers of the Realm* (1953)
  The Age of Chivalry (1963)
Bushell, Thomas *The Sage of Salisbury, Thomas Chubb* (1968)
Cobbett, William *Rural Rides*
Dorling, E. E. *A History of Salisbury* (1911)
Farrant, J. P. *The History of Scout Motors Limited* (1967)
Fletcher, J. M. J. *Notes on Salisbury Cathedral* (1924)
Haskins, C. *The Ancient Trade Guilds and Companies of Salisbury* (1912)
Hudson, W. H. *A Shepherd's Life* (1910)
Ivie, John *Declaration* (1661)
Jowitt, R. L. P. *Salisbury* (1951)
Massingham, H. J. *English Downland* (1936)
Northy, T. J. *The Popular History of Old & New Sarum* (1897)
Noyes, Ella *Salisbury Plain* (1913)
Plumb, J. H. *England in the Eighteenth Century* (1950)
Pope, Walter *Life of Seth, Lord Bishop of Salisbury* ed. Bamborough (1961)
Robertson, Dora H. *Sarum Close* (1938)
Shortt, Hugh (ed.) *City of Salisbury* (1957)
  Salisbury (1972)
Smethurst, A. F. *Salisbury Cathedral* (1976)
Stenton, D. M. *English Society in the Early Middle Ages* (1951)
Stratford, Joseph *Wiltshire and its Worthies* (1882)
Summers, J. H. *George Herbert* (1954)
Symons, Geraldine *Children in the Close* (1959)
The Salisbury Times
The Salisbury Journal
Thomas, Hugh *Salisbury Plain*
Trevelyan, G. M. *Illustrated English Social History* (1949–52)
The Victoria County History of Wiltshire, Vol. III Pugh (ed.) (1956)
  Vol. IV Pugh (ed.) (1959)
  Vol. VI Crittall (ed.) (1962)
Walls, Ernest *The Salisbury Avon* (1929)
Walton, Isaak *The Works of George Herbert in Prose and Verse, containing
  'The Life of Mr George Herbert'*
Wordsworth, C. *Sarum Processions and Ceremonies* (1901)
Ziegler, Philip *The Black Death* (1969)
The Dictionary of National Biography

Index